PERFECT EVERY TIME

When Doing It All
Leaves You with Nothing...

PAULA RINEHART

D1056094

NAVPRESS
BRINGING TRUTH TO LIFE
NavPress Publishing Group
P.O. Box 35001, Colorado Springs, Colorado 80935

The Navigators is an international Christian organization. Jesus Christ gave His followers the Great Commission to go and make disciples (Matthew 28:19). The aim of The Navigators is to help fulfill that commission by multiplying laborers for Christ in every nation.

NavPress is the publishing ministry of The Navigators. NavPress publications are tools to help Christians grow. Although publications alone cannot make disciples or change lives, they can help believers learn biblical discipleship, and apply what they learn to their lives and ministries.

Library of Congress Catalog Card Number: 92-31969
ISBN 08910-97082

The stories in this book come from the lives of real women. Facts and situations have been changed to protect their identity. Any resemblance to people living or dead is coincidental.

Unless otherwise identified, all Scripture in this publication is from the *Holy Bible: New International Version* (NIV). Copyright © 1973, 1978, 1984, International Bible Society. Used by permission of Zondervan Bible Publishers. Another version used is the *New American Standard Bible* (NASB), © The Lockman Foundation 1960, 1962, 1963, 1968, 1971, 1972, 1973, 1975, 1977.

Rinehart, Paula.
  Perfect every time : when doing it all leaves you with nothing / Paula Rinehart.
    p. cm.
  Includes bibliographical references.
  ISBN 0-89109-708-2 : $10.00
  1. Women – United States – Psychology.   2. Stress (Psychology) – United States.   3. Performance – Psychological aspects.   I. Title.
HQ1206.R56   1992
155.6'33 – dc20   92-31969
                                                                   CIP

Printed in the United States of America

FOR A FREE CATALOG OF
NAVPRESS BOOKS & BIBLE STUDIES,
CALL TOLL FREE 1-800-366-7788 (USA)
or 1-416-499-4615 (CANADA)

C O N T E N T S

To Jennifer,
with gratitude for the privilege
of living shared lives

❦

"But for you who fear My name
the sun of righteousness will rise
with healing in its wings;
and you will go forth and skip
about like calves from the stall."
MALACHI 4:2

ACKNOWLEDGMENTS

Writing a book always seems, to me at least, a lot like having a baby. The relief of finally seeing that child whole and in one piece almost makes you forget the long months of anticipation and waiting.

But when I think about the actual process of writing this book, I am reminded of the many people who've influenced me along the way. I am especially indebted to Traci Mullins, my editor and friend, who helped me give shape and substance to my thoughts and challenged me to share my own journey in it all. Most of all, she has given me courage. To Brent, Jennifer, and Maureen I am grateful for their perceptive insights and listening ear; to Alma Young, Holly Miller, Meg Lynch, Leslie Martin, Lise Piden, Dianna Green, and Rhonda Garrett for their willingness to share their stories with me; to Dr. Peter Dyck for his help and insight; to Carolyn Hill, Lynn Bartholomew, Jennifer Ennis, Maggie Wynne, and Alma Young who read and offered suggestions on this manuscript.

My husband, Stacy, has given me what I most needed over the last few years—the time and willingness to help me sort through both the questions and, at times, the painful confusion that change brings. To him, my deepest thanks.

My hope is that you, as the reader, will hear your own voice spoken in the stories of women related in this book and that in their stories you will find a measure of your own.

FOREWORD

Having known Paula Rinehart for nearly twenty years, I have had the pleasure of growing close to her as a friend and simultaneously enjoying the opportunity to observe the deepening in her Christian walk and the burgeoning of her skills as a writer. As a wife and mother and one who is extremely active in ministries to women, Paula brings a wide breadth of knowledge and experience to the subject of perfectionism and personal "drivenness." She writes with a clear capacity to see through the facades that lock us in the mental and behavioral patterns of perfectionism.

Paula writes with a gentle ease and precision that positions the reader to visualize with uncommon clarity the images and insights that might otherwise slip past us. She reveals the overall scope of the subject while not failing to miss those vital details and anecdotes that enrich the core of her book. She leads us to search beyond the "whats" and "whens" of our all-too-hurried lives, and beautifully guides us to focus on the deeper "whys" that are buried behind behaviors.

From the recounting of her own encounter with physical maladies and the subsequent dealing with physical and emotional burnout, Paula draws a clear and penetrating view of the incessant and insidiously costly inner drive to be the quintessential achiever. With a plethora of examples and insights, she substantiates that "all real 'doing' in life must first be grounded in 'being.'"

It is a heady, often painful journey on which she leads the reader, but well worth the labor. From the pages of her work emerges an increasingly clear message of inescapable truth and a hope that challenges toward change. Her insight and practical options not only illuminate the path, but make real change possible. She has often conveyed to me the belief that "mere words don't change people, decisions do." This book is much more than a review of what we previously knew about perfectionism. Rather, it is a compelling, enthralling excursion into areas of depth within the feminine soul. I heartily recommend this book to women who are perfectionists and to those who think they are not.

—WALTER R. BYRD, M.D.

PART · ONE

*Profiles
of Women
Who Do Too Much*

CHAPTER ONE

A Journey I Never Intended to Make: An Unnerving Invitation to Sanity

For your name's sake, O LORD, preserve my life;
in your righteousness, bring me out of trouble.
PSALM 143:11

I was driving down the freeway in early autumn, late for an appointment, when the first strange rumblings in my chest began. Little bursts of pain—it felt like someone was pinching me from the inside.

This will go away if I ignore it, I reasoned. *It's like a headache, only in a different place. All I need are a couple of aspirins and a diet Coke.* I kept driving.

But the chest pain didn't go away. It seemed to have a mind of its own, continuing to appear from out of nowhere—even in the middle of the night—and then disappear for no reason. As the days wore on, I varied in my private self-diagnoses. None of them could be cured by an aspirin. Was this an ulcer, a tumor, the first warnings of a heart attack? Whatever it was, I knew that chest pain was not on the list of common maladies for a woman of thirty-five. I was supposed to be running track and having babies, not heart attacks.

Reluctantly, I carved out a spot on my calendar to visit the doctor.

I had hoped that he would have a quick and easy

explanation, even a prescription that I could take for ten days like a case of strep throat. Instead, I learned that chest pain is an invitation for a host of medical tests. He wanted my chest x-rayed, my heart valves studied, my stomach surveyed. Even my gall bladder would not escape his scrutiny.

I groaned when I thought of the time lost sitting in stray waiting rooms, but all I said was, "Let's get it over with. I have a lot of work to do."

A month later I found myself back in his office with the same chest pain, hoping for answers. He read me the test results, all of which were absurdly normal. "I don't understand," I said finally. "I still have chest pain. We've tested everything from my nose to my navel and yet there's no reason for the pain?"

At that point the doctor laid the lab results aside and leaned back in his chair like a grandfather ready to light his pipe. He addressed my question with one of his own. "What's happening in your life these days?" he asked. "Are you under a lot of pressure?"

How do you answer a question like that? I thought. *Isn't everyone under a lot of pressure?* I would rather he had stuck to the subject of gall bladders and x-rays.

"No more than usual," I answered in a tentative voice. "My youngest is in kindergarten. I'm writing a book. My husband travels frequently. I had a miscarriage last summer. Fairly normal stuff." I hoped my answer would satisfy him quickly.

But something stirred in his eyes, and he leaned forward to look straight at me with a prophet's gaze. "Paula," he said, "I suspect you have been burning the candle at both ends for a long time. I see it all the time in women like you. You have a home and children and extended family and all sorts of responsibilities. There's no end to it. Your body won't keep up this kind of pace. Something will have to give.

"I think I know the cause of your chest pain. It's a little word called *stress*. Perhaps you need to slow down."

I left the doctor's office that day with mixed feelings. On one hand, I was relieved. At least I wasn't dying . . . not immediately, anyway. But in another sense, I felt my body was betraying me. I had lived at an incredible pace all my years, and deep down, I was proud of it. A full "do-list" was a call to arms for me. I guess some part of me felt that a calendar with empty spaces and a phone that didn't ring were proof of not being much in demand. And yet my body was clearly refusing to cooperate. I felt like the captain of a ship whose crew had threatened mutiny.

"Slow down," the doctor had said. I tried his words on for size like a dress that was too expensive to consider buying. *A slower, saner life.* For a few brief moments the prospect almost looked inviting. I had visions of reading a novel for no good reason on my back porch with the Colorado afternoon sun warming the pages.

But the notion of a slower lifestyle was also pretty frightening. What on earth would I do with myself if I wasn't doing all I was doing?

❦

In the end, I kept right on going, for a couple of years anyway. I found that you can ignore chest pain fairly easily if you no longer fear heart failure. In time, it almost goes away.

Yet nagging little questions continued to surface over and over in a way I could no longer ignore. Something was shifting inside me, like giant templates on the ocean floor. I knew, in my stiller moments, that I needed to pay attention.

One thing I found confusing was that the "stress" in my life was the accumulation of so many good things. Our two children were growing up, and while they needed rides to soccer and a lot of dialogue, at least they could brush their own teeth now. That left room for other people's needs in bigger ways. My husband was directing a leadership program in a Christian organization, and slowly, I picked up small groups to lead and people to help and counsel. In between, I sandwiched the research and study necessary in order to continue to write. Living in the hectic environment of the organization's headquarters location meant that there were always unexpected people to see, one more lunch to squeeze into a crowded schedule. My calendar was filled, for the most part, with good things. What could be the problem?

The problem was that the busier I got, the more empty I felt. And my response to that emptiness was to gear up and try a bit harder. Perhaps a more consistent devotional life would restore my motivation. Maybe the next book I read would hold a secret that I had overlooked. I thumbed through women's magazines in search of new time-management tips. But the feeling that something more basic was amiss wouldn't go away.

In moments of honesty, I began to wonder if there wasn't an exit off this merry-go-round. I was getting tired—tired of watching life go by in a blur. I found myself wondering what it would really take for me to slow down. *What was behind all that doing?*

Could it be, perhaps, that my chest pain was God's special invitation to explore my lifelong pattern of driving so hard? Was I being given, in my inner unrest and physical symptoms, the opportunity to get at the emotional roots of my inability to say "no"?

THE NEED TO ACHIEVE

Like many women, I come from a long line of "doers": great-grandmothers of English, Scottish, and German stock who carved a life out of a rugged wilderness. Women whose day always began early and ended late. Women who lived unconsciously by the motto "Nothing comes—all must be fetched." There was no such thing as waiting around for life to happen, no time for just being. You might get left behind.

Now many generations later, that "doing" emphasis was part of the warp and woof of my life. It was always a challenge to me to see how many things I could do at once. With a little juggling, I could fix dinner, supervise homework, watch the news—and give advice to a friend on the phone. Long phone cords were made for women like me.

When my children were small, my daughter and I invented a little snap-clap sequence that we applied to oncoming red lights. Magically, that red light would turn green! And if it didn't, you just had to repeat the trick until it did. I hated to slow down for anything. It's easy to see why one of my daughter's very first words was "hurry."

Where was I going in such a rush? Why was I pushing so hard? All that "doing" in my life took many shapes and forms. One of those was the perennial need to feel I was achieving something. I could not just write a paper for a class; I had to write an exceptional paper. A splendid one. If leading one Bible study was good, then leading two was all the better. If someone could have taken a look deep inside me I think they might have found Descartes' words transposed on the walls of my heart: "I do, therefore I am."

The drive to go and do and achieve and please permeated many aspects of my life. Memories, long buried, began to surface as though someone were preparing a court case against the way I had been living. One that was representative of many others stood out in my mind, like a scene inside a bell jar.

After a full afternoon into which the children and I had packed as much as possible, I found my daughter, Allison, outside on the front porch swing with her sneakers and pigtails bouncing in the cool breeze. She was eight at the time. When she saw me she got this big electric smile on her dirty little face, and she said, "Hey, Mom, come sit here beside me."

I put down a sack of groceries and complied with her request, and we started to swing. Yet as I did, a nonsensical question slipped out of my mouth. "What do you want me to *do* for you?" I asked, as though there must be some hidden point to this activity.

She looked at me and cocked her head as her own question. "Nothing," she said. "Just sit here with me and swing." It was the simple request of a child, but it knocked me off balance. I did what she asked, but I'm not sure that on the inside I ever really sat down.

That was characteristic of the way I lived—always three steps ahead of the present moment. I might sit in the swing with Allison, for instance, but I was not really there with her. I was thinking about something else, usually the next thing that needed to be done.

When you live in the future you are always internally in motion, moving toward the next achievement, the next need to be met. You can be months, even years, ahead of yourself. It's a "when I finish . . . then" approach to life where real living is put on hold. Yet I found, ironically, that when I did reach the next juncture—when I finished the degree or delivered the baby or wrote the article—I couldn't enjoy that either. It slid off me like water on a duck's back. I was mentally way down the road.

A VICIOUS CYCLE

As I considered my compelling tendency to overdo and my inability to say "no," I realized there was a pattern to my habits.

As long as I was immersed in a project or moving

toward a goal, life had meaning and purpose. But as soon as a blank space appeared or my schedule eased up, I was more anxious than relieved. And the only way to address the anxiety, it seemed, was to get busy again. The illusion was that some inner blessing awaited me just around the corner. Another degree, another book written, always the next accomplishment promised to put me over the top. Then I could relax.

After one experience in particular I began to see myself as a willing, even if unhappy, participant in a vicious cycle. I had always wanted to have an article published in a favorite magazine—one I frequently read that rarely published contributions by women. As usual, I worked hard, doing enough raw research to justify writing a book instead of an article. I even dented the front fender of the car while hurrying to an interview. In the end, though, they published the article.

When I first found out my article had been accepted, I was elated. But the excitement lasted all of thirty minutes. When I went back to my office, there was just a blank computer screen to face, another article or chapter to be written. The sense of euphoria was not portable. In thirty minutes' time, I had gone from Cinderella in her ball gown to Cinderella in her housecoat.

Even success left me empty, as empty as if I had never set out to accomplish the goal in the first place. *Why was the pleasure so short-lived?* I wondered. The external applause I counted on was beginning to do less for me—like a drug that continual use renders less effective. There was a hollow spot on the inside that seemed strangely untouched by anyone, even God.

The questions that stirred in me as the result of my bout with chest pain were leading me to some startling revelations. I saw that doing—or the relentless need to achieve and to please—was something that could be just as addicting as any contraband substance. It spoke of an inner vacuum, a desperate attempt to "fill up" an insatiable space within.

All my overdoing provided me with a "fix" that protected me from having to face myself.

GOD AND GRACE

Now the natural question to ask at this point in my story would be, "Where was God in all of this?" After all, for the past twenty years—or half of my lifetime—the fact that I was a Christian had been the governing principle of my life . . . or so I thought.

My spiritual journey began in the late sixties, during that window of time when the big emphasis was on the Great Commission and reaching the world for Christ. Strangely enough, my love affair with perpetual motion fit quite well into evangelical Christianity. I felt right at home as I learned to study the Bible and share the gospel and manage time down to fifteen-minute intervals. The Great Commission was a task to be accomplished. While it was mammoth, at least the goal was clear.

If someone had asked me, I could have defended the doctrine of being "saved by grace" like a trial lawyer. God had brought me into a relationship with Him through no effort of my own. I knew that much. It was not a question of what I had done, but what God had done for me that counted. Somehow, though, that marvelous theology failed to carry over into the way I approached life. The way I lived shouted clearly that what I really believed was this: the great weight of following Christ rested squarely on my shoulders.

Being a Christian somehow heightened my drive to reach superhuman goals. It was as though I had placed an overlay on top of Scripture that highlighted in neon color the verses about discipline and personal effort. If there were thirty things wrong with my life, then with

God's help, perhaps I could narrow the gap to twenty. And if I really applied myself, another ten might be taken off the list. Those who were the most spiritually mature were the ones who had come closest to the goal of being "fixed." They had it all together.

It seemed as though, if you really wanted God's involvement with you, you needed to be hard at work for Him. Experiencing His power meant, somehow, being given the ability to live beyond any personal limitations. I could keep going and doing and giving out to others because, if the goals were worthy, God would come to my rescue. A woman with a deep spiritual commitment would never fail to respond to the pressing needs around her. What I lacked, especially, was God's permission to take life at a more realistic, human pace.

I remember reading about a woman who spent a harried week directing sixth graders in a vacation Bible school, rushing through activities, games, and field trips that had taken almost a month to plan. On the last day, after all the kids were gone, she found herself on her hands and knees scraping papier-mâché off the floor with a knife and talking to herself. "I sure hope God appreciates all this," she muttered.[1]

I smiled when I read the candor in her response. She expressed the same driven effort to please I felt, an effort that spilled over into my relationship with God.

The story of Mary and Martha entertaining Jesus in their home was a familiar one, and of course, I knew I fit the profile of Martha. I knew how hard it was to stop all that motion. I knew how easily a task became paramount.

Yet something in me also longed to hang up my towel, serve store-bought dessert, and join Mary. *"That's enough. You've done enough. Come sit here with us."* My ears strained to hear words like those, but they seemed meant for someone else. I tried to find the "off" button inside me, but I couldn't reach the switch.

I was discovering that there were significant parts of me that had yet to hear the good news of the gospel.

A FEAR OF INADEQUACY

So experiencing recurring chest pain was something like a referee's whistle, a yellow flag thrown down on the field of play. When I look back on my life prior to the pain, I sometimes wonder why it never occurred to me to stop and examine how I was living. I see the amazing grace of God in bringing me up short.

Over the course of a few years, this was a process that felt as though the outer layer of my life was being peeled away—stripped, in front of my eyes. I began to see the hidden motivations and secret fears that lay beneath the polish and pleasant appearance.

From any angle, the question of vital concern had always been how well I performed. Had I said the right words to a troubled friend? Were my children getting enough vitamins and books read to them and manners learned? Did I have what it took to keep my husband happy? Was God pleased with me? Had I done enough? Life contained a series of tasks, the successful completion of which was a running commentary on my adequacy as a woman—as a Christian.

This came home to me one day when my mother sent a present through the mail. "You won't believe what I picked up for you today," she had said when she called. "I'm sending it as a surprise."

When I unwrapped the package, those were the first words out of my mouth. "You're right, Mom. I don't believe this." For there in the tissue paper lay a padded bra. A seriously padded bra. A padded bra with enough stuffing for a throw pillow on my couch! Though I empathized with my mother's effort to fill out my clothes, I had to laugh when I thought of actually trying to wear this.

But then, before I had the chance to put the bra back in the tissue paper, a thought struck me that had little to do with the gift itself. What I saw in the box was the message about myself I had always intuitively believed: *Somehow I didn't have enough. I didn't have what it took.* And if I didn't work very hard to camouflage that reality with some sort of good showing, someone would discover the awful truth.

Whether it was writing an article or teaching a simple class, I had no mental category called "giving it my best shot." Whatever effort it took to perform well—really well—was effort well spent. In grade school I sometimes set my alarm for three a.m., just to get up and check to see that I had every piece of my homework and that it was done right. Only then could I sleep in peace. That pattern followed me all my life. In my way of thinking, someone who'd had braces on her teeth, eight years of ballet, and her college education paid for should not grow up to be average. *Average* was a dirty word. Average was conspicuously close to the word *failure.*

An inner critic lived with me, like a black crow perched on my shoulder, always evaluating. "Do better, do better, do better," it cawed, prodding me onward. I no sooner completed a project than I began immediately to judge its worth. Somehow if I just tried hard enough I might discover the one missing secret that would drive back forever those feelings of inadequacy.

The object was to win, to succeed—but to win what? What was the carrot on the end of the stick? Everyone loves a winner, that I knew. Those were the rules to life, but the operative word was the verb *loves.* Everyone loves a winner, so though I longed to be declared good enough just as I was, I had to keep pushing ahead. Somewhere, early on, I had adopted the belief that *people who do the best are loved the most.*

Aiming at some form of success seemed like reason

enough to stay on the treadmill. That is, until one summer of discontent, when I began to recognize that treadmill of overachieving for what it really was: the bars of a self-imposed prison.

Two or three events converged together that summer—new challenges for which I might have risen to the occasion, at another point in my life. My husband changed jobs, requiring a reorientation for me in terms of the role I played. Our best friends decided to move back east. Suddenly, our calendar was much emptier. My youngest child was struggling much too hard to learn to read, and I didn't know how to help him. But I seemed to have no energy, whatever, to face any of these things.

A deep fatigue settled into my body. And my mind, normally restless and active, ground to a halt.

I went through the motions of appearing in the right places, doing and saying the right things. But I felt as though I were speaking through a plate glass window, and had someone possibly peeked around the edge, they would have found no one there. I continued to read my Bible, and though the words were familiar, they seemed lifeless. All the music was gone. I stifled the urge to say, "So what? I have forgotten the point."

This is strange, I thought, *I don't remember feeling this way before.* I found myself staring into the mirror to make sure I was still there. The reflection was the same, my skin was warm, my make-up in place. That was hard to believe, though, because on the inside I felt dead.

I felt like I had died, but I hadn't gone to Heaven.

AN INVITATION

My summer of depression, marked by burnout, deep fatigue, and the feeling of being brain-dead, is a frighteningly common outcome for women who are caught in some form of a performance trap.

All of us who recognize ourselves as a woman "who does too much" hold this characteristic in common: We rarely realize how close to the edge we live until we have almost stepped over the line. We don't start to read the messages on the wall until we have painted ourselves into a corner. We are too busy—doing too much.

No matter how high your energy level, you can give for only so long without adequate replenishment. The well eventually goes dry. It is God's way of puncturing the myth that you can make it on your own as a strong, independent woman who has no needs herself.

That summer was God's way of getting my attention, and as such, I felt as though He had taken my hand and invited me on a journey, an inner journey. I found that I had to discover the emotional roots of my tendency to overdo. There were reasons beneath my behavior that kept me locked in place, responding reflexively like a puppet on cue. As I discovered more of those internal dynamics, I became freer to choose another path.

What came as a result were many good things—a joy in receiving from the Lord and from other people, an inner release that gave me permission to be more of the woman God had made me. Sometimes I have to force myself to remember how awful that summer was, because life seems very different now.

But then, I'm getting way ahead of the story.

NOTE

1. Sue Monk Kidd, *God's Joyful Surprise* (San Francisco: Harper & Row, 1987), page 15.

CHAPTER TWO

Standing on Our Mothers' Shoulders: Reaching for the Stars

*I would have despaired unless I had believed
that I would see the goodness of the LORD
in the land of the living.*
PSALM 27:13, NASB

I share my story with you because I suspect that I am not alone in this phenomenon of being a woman who does too much. If I held that distinction by myself, I guess I would confine my writing to my journals. But the elements inherent in my story—perfectionism, fear of failure, feelings of inadequacy, a compelling need to please—are only too descriptive of the lives of multitudes of women as our culture moves through the nineties.

It's easy to wonder, sometimes, if there really is more pressure on women today. Do we really have more to contend with than our mothers and grandmothers did?

I think of my own grandmother, who raised eleven children in the mountains of Virginia, ran a general store, canned all her own food, and wrung the neck of the chicken that would appear on her Sunday dinner table. She was no stranger to hard work. No doubt there were too many demands on her time and energy.

Yet I have to admit that there are significant differences in her day and mine—in her day and ours. My grandmother had live-in "hired help" to lift the load. She didn't feel discontent because her bedrooms weren't coordinated with Waverly fabrics. No specialist told her to read to her children in utero or to brush their teeth while they were still nestled under the gums.

She lived in an era when front porches were made for sitting and Sunday afternoons were saved for "visitin'" with the neighbors. In spite of all she had to do, hers was a slower, saner time when there were built-in breathing spells that allowed the soul to catch up with the body. What she chose to replenish herself was quite common for the women of her day. In spite of all she had to do, you could find her out in the back yard early on any given morning in a big straw hat. She was tending her flower garden. There amid gladioli and chrysanthemums she carved a little spot of quietness and beauty. In her day and time, people understood more instinctively that all real "doing" in life must first be grounded in "being."

I am the first to admit that there is no going back to grandmother's day. Any Virginia Slims commercial reminds you of that fact: "You've come a long way, baby." Women now chair a board meeting or change a flat tire or teach their children to read before kindergarten—or try to do all these things.

In fact, if anything, we are the victims of our own success. It is precisely because there are so *many* opportunities accessible to us that our lives are more stress-ridden than those of our mothers and grandmothers.

Our hands are full of briefcases and diaper bags, Sunday school lessons and notes for a PTA fund-raiser. So full, in fact, that we resemble a character in a novel I read who, when confronted with bills he couldn't pay, simply dropped the whole stack from the top of his basement steps and paid the ones that landed closest to him! The claims on his money were more than he had the resources to meet adequately. In a similar way, women today face both more opportunities and more demands on them than they can choose between.

My point is that, if we are ever to get to the bottom of what it is that makes us women who are perennially given to "overdoing," then we must acknowledge the cultural pressures that feed our predisposition to overdo.

There are at least a couple of compelling reasons why being a woman is a more confusing and stress-filled adventure now than at any other time in this century.

DISTORTED MODELS OF THE IDEAL WOMAN

There was a time when a woman could consider her life a success if she kept a clean house, hot food on the table, her husband's shirts ironed, and her children healthy. Being a homemaker was a completely respectable profession. To excel in the nurturing abilities that women have always been known for—being a good wife, mother, and friend—was good enough.

Women emerged from the sixties, though, with both the opportunity and the mandate to be more. Many of the doors were that flung open to them had been traditionally reserved for men. All of a sudden, or so it seemed, it was no longer enough to create a home and cook a mean plate of lasagna, or to care for your children in your own back yard. There were big worlds "out there" to conquer.

One way the changing definition of being a woman can be demonstrated is in the quiet revolution that took place in the world of "doll babies." Thirty years ago, for the first time, a doll that wasn't a baby was introduced to little girls. Barbie burst on the scene as a sophisticated teenager who recruited her fans with this slogan: "We girls can do anything; right, Barbie?!"

She was a "doll baby" that skipped childhood altogether. She came complete with silky hair and a perfect female shape. And for thirty years, she has never aged, never wrinkled. Her boyfriend, Ken, still comes to get her in a pink sports car. She is Murphy Brown in a doll with just the right clothes for work and home and play. Most of all, Barbie won't ever be caught wetting her pants—or shedding any real tears. She is perfect.

Barbie was one forerunner of the woman with unlimited potential—the woman who could do it all. As such, she did not so much shape our views of what a real woman was as she simply modeled a set of ideas already in the wind.

For more than three decades, the message that has been incubating in the hearts of women is, if you just try hard enough you, too, should be able to do it all. Today we have culled the major characteristics of women and men and wed them together to create an unreachable ideal, a superwoman. "Many women today, whose chosen life-style is a major departure from that of their mothers, are trying to emulate both their parents," writes Ellen Sue Stern in her book about female stress. "They strive to fulfill their idea of the perfect mother *and father*, expecting themselves to create a home and maintain warm, personal relationships while simultaneously developing careers and making their mark."[1]

The illusion is that a real woman should be able to juggle both roles at the same time and keep it all going smoothly. The expectation is for her to follow in the footsteps of men, even if she has to walk doubletime in heels with a two-year-old clinging to her skirt. She flips through *Savvy* magazine and concludes that since she hasn't started her own business yet and she is still with her first husband she must be a failure.

She internalizes the messages about what a real woman is and an unconscious conviction takes shape inside her. *If I can't do it all, then there is something wrong with me.* When you consider the role overload many of us function under, it is not surprising that the suicide rate for women over the age of thirty-five is reported to be three times that of men.

As women have increasingly made themselves at home in the world of achievement and outer success, our lives have taken on the same pressures that men have—who weren't meant to live this way either. In terms of drivenness, we have unknowingly mimicked men, becoming more and more a part of "the cult of busyness."[2] The rites of this cult suggest that unless you are rushed and stretched to the limit, stuck in perpetual motion, there is something wrong with you. Like people operating on remote control, we end up going through all the motions long after we've forgotten the point.

Too often, an understanding of what God desires for our lives gets tangled in our own misconceptions of the distorted ideal of being superwoman. God is seen as the source of power, enabling us to face an endless string of responsibilities and demands. The hope of experiencing His favor becomes, in a tragic way, one more reason to try so hard, to give so much. We lack His permission and encouragement to take life slower, more sanely.

It is not so much that women today are neither male nor female, but that they feel the pressure to be androgynous, to be like *both*. Mother, wife, homemaker *and* butcher, baker, candlestick maker. The sad part is that in assuming the traits of both, we wind up relinquishing some of the ground of what it means to be a woman who can be touched and enjoyed as a *woman*. In her book *Being a Woman*, Dr. Toni Grant points out that when "women become masculine and men become feminine, each takes on the worst traits of the other. Men take on a woman's softness without her strength; women take on a man's toughness without his kindness."[3]

In reality, we have at our fingertips, in our innate feminine natures, part of what is needed to restore and maintain balance in our lives.

By femininity, I am not speaking of a list of specific duties or a particular way to look. The issues at stake are more fundamental, having to do with our essential way of relating to life. Perhaps the key word central to our identity as women is *relationships* or *relatedness*. After years of study into the feminine psyche, Harvard researcher Carol Gilligan has concluded that, no matter what they do in life, most women's sense of identity is forged in the context of their relationships.[4] Even the female anatomy mirrors back to us this reality. We have the capacity to conceive and nourish life, and somehow this nourishing, life-giving quality is an intrinsic part of true feminine strength.

The deeper a woman delves into her own capacity for relatedness, the more she will discover the essential keys that unlock the hold of drivenness and performance-based living on her life.

When drivenness and compulsive activity pervade our lives, it is because the pendulum has swung away from the best parts of our femaleness toward the mutation of a false masculine emphasis. Our truest energies are drained with all the effort it takes to maintain the feverish pace.

OPPORTUNITIES OUR MOTHERS
ONLY DREAMED ABOUT

Another factor in the pressure that women feel and our tendency to do too much is that we carry on our shoulders the hopes and dreams of generations of women before us.

"My mother married quite young," a middle-aged editor explains about her life, "and she always wanted to write. I think I always sensed her 'what if?' It was almost as if I wanted to pick up where she left off." She cites the chance to become what her mother couldn't as a large factor in the drivenness of her twenties and thirties.

In many ways, this woman's words describe what many of us today have done with our lives: We have picked up where our mothers left off. Doors that were closed to women, even a generation ago, are swinging wide open these days. "I feel the weight of the dreams of two generations of women on my shoulders," admits a mother of two who teaches on the college level. "My grandmother used to pull me aside when I was quite young and coach me: 'Sarah, don't be the nurse, be the doctor. Don't be the secretary, be the lawyer.' My mother and my grandmother were smart, capable women. Their message to me was clear: 'You have opportunities I could only dream of—you must not fail me.'"

To us it befell both the chance—and the urgency—to make up for the lost time and missed opportunities of prior generations. Sarah Hardesty and Nehama Jacobs, who wrote a widely received book on successful women and the stress in their lives, claim that most women's concept of achievement is formed by their mother's influence, rather than their father's.[5] That is understandable when you consider how naturally mothers look to their daughters for an image of who they were—and what they might have become. Through their daughters they would be able to taste a wider experience of life than they had been able to know.

Given where we stand poised in the latter part of this century—reaching from the shoulders of our mothers and grandmothers, so to speak—we naturally feel the pressure to answer an unspoken question: What have we made of those opportunities? What have we made of our lives?

TWO KINDS OF WOMEN

I have just described some of the external reasons why women "who do too much" do too much. In the remaining parts of this book we will focus more on the inner world of women who are caught in a trap of performance, of trying to be perfect. While the release from those pressures—both inner and outer—is something that God seeks to accomplish in our lives from the inside out, it is important that we admit, up front, that ours is a day of great expectations on women. We need to know what we're up against.

Two kinds of overdoing in women form the focus of this book. The first is the "push-ahead woman" who invests a significantly high portion of her life in reaching goals and proving her competence. She is driven to perform well. Only by some sort of applause or recognition can she feel that she is somebody. Her fragile sense of worth is directly attached to abilities and achievements.

As women have entered the work place, this kind of woman has become more and more prevalent. The work environment, in many ways, fosters whatever latent tendencies we possess to feel the need to prove ourselves. It rewards success and punishes failure. The outer stress and inner emptiness that have plagued men for years are becoming increasingly common for women.

The second type of performance trap this book will address is that of "the indispensable woman." In some ways, this kind of excessive doing appears, on the surface, to be more "feminine" because the focus of the indispensable woman's effort is *people*. Her nurturing abilities are channeled into helping, fixing, and pleasing the people in her life. This is her mark of personal achievement, so to speak, and the means by which she measures her value.

Many women who can't say no will find that elements of both kinds of women characterize their lives. They may "major" in being a push-ahead woman and "minor" in being an indispensable one, or vice versa. Others will be able to spot quickly that they fit the profile of one or the other, but not both.

In either case, it is important to recognize that we are talking about a pattern of living that is chronic, not acute. These tendencies have usually been in place for years. As we age, they are fed from an increasing number of sources:

our past, cultural expectations, a false understanding of God and His favor, our own unmet needs. All of these build like the crescendo of an inner orchestra, until we are forced to admit that dissonant cymbals are clanging in our ears, demanding to be heard.

Although this book will address, in general, the inner pressures that drive a woman toward a lifestyle of doing too much, you will find it helpful to pinpoint which type of overdoing you are most prone toward. Your responses to the following questions will help you discover whether or not your life is characterized by significant measures of one or both drives.

Simply answer each question with a "yes" or a "no" and tally up the number of times you answered "yes" in each category.[6]

Evaluation Questions—A

1. Do you have trouble saying "no" to others even when you know you should?

2. When people in your life are bored or unhappy, do you think you need to do something about it?

3. Do you often feel overwhelmed with your schedule?

4. Do you ask questions about other people's lives, but find they seldom ask about yours?

5. Do you feel guilty when you say "no"? *sometimes*

6. Do you spend a fair amount of time trying to steer your friends and family away from negative influences?

7. Do you hesitate to tell others the truth for fear they may be hurt or offended? *yes*

8. Do you wonder why so many people lean on you?

9. Do you find yourself feeling guilty or responsible for others' poor choices in life?

10. Do you say "it doesn't matter," even when it really does?

11. Do you often hear yourself apologizing for something?

12. When others ask how you're doing, do you usually answer "fine," no matter what's happening?

13. Do you wonder "who you are"?

14. When an unexpected need arises, do you usually do your best to move your schedule around to accommodate it?

15. Is your first inclination to say "no" when something fun comes up?

16. Do you believe that life is mostly "struggle" and "duty"?

17. If you went away for a week, would the closest people in your life find it quite difficult to function?

18. Even when others offer their help or support, do you usually find a way to "do it yourself"?

19. Do you feel it's your place to "take whatever's left"?

20. Do you believe that you work harder than those around you?

Evaluation Questions—B

1. Are you often amazed at the incompetence of other people?

2. Does it seem like others expect a lot from you?

3. Is "failure" hard for you to accept? *yes*

4. Do you have many acquaintances, but few intimate friends? *yes*

5. Are you perennially trying to plan for the next step in life, the next goal?

6. When you excel in one area of your life, do you frequently worry whether you'll be able to do the same again?

7. Do you look at women with average jobs and enough spare time and wonder how they can settle for mediocrity?

8. Are you chronically prone to compare your own performance with others? *yes*

9. If all your responsibilities magically disappeared, would you feel empty and aimless? *anxious*

10. Do you often think that if you only had a little more time you could get everything done?

11. Do you frequently feel impatient at others' mistakes or poor judgment?

12. Does it take more than a little while for you to recover from criticism? *yes!*

13. Is your best rarely good enough in your own eyes? *yes*

14. Does success make you feel pressured to do even more? *yes*

15. Are you afraid that significant people in your life will someday "discover" you aren't as talented and capable as they seem to think?

16. Do you ever feel empty and hollow as though you were just a shell of a person?

17. Do others' compliments seem to "roll right off you"?

18. Do you find yourself unable to say "no" to more work?

19. Would your face turn red if friends or coworkers caught you in a situation that signified "weakness" to you? *yes*

20. Do most of your relationships feel professional and distant? *yes*

If you answered "yes" to more than seven questions in either set or a total of more than twelve in both, then there is a strong likelihood that your life reflects the patterns and impediments of a woman who does too much.

The first set of questions reflects some of the characteristics and inner feelings of *the indispensable woman*. The questions in the second set reflect those of *the push-ahead woman*. By comparing your scores in both sets you will be able to see which tendency is strongest for you.

If you answered "yes" to more than five questions in each set, then you likely feel torn in numerous directions.

You may need to put this book down and head immediately for the Bahamas! If you can't arrange that, then perhaps a highlight pen or some underlining will help.

In the next two chapters, we will explore more deeply the profiles of these two kinds of women—their struggles, their fears, and their untapped potential.

NOTES
1. Ellen Sue Stern, *The Indispensable Woman* (Toronto: Bantam Books, 1988), page 64.
2. Amy Saltzman, *Downshifting* (New York: Harper Collins, 1991), page 20.
3. Dr. Toni Grant, *Being a Woman: Fulfilling Your Femininity and Finding Love* (New York: Avon Books, 1988), page 57.
4. Carol Gilligan, as quoted by Dr. Larry Crabb in *Men and Women: Enjoying the Difference* (Grand Rapids: Zondervan, 1991), page 161.
5. Sarah Hardesty and Nehama Jacobs, *Success and Betrayal* (New York: Franklin Watts, 1986), page 24.
6. These questions are compiled from a variety of sources with special credit given to Dennis and Marilyn Chambon's seminar on interpersonal relationships, Colorado Springs, Colorado, 1989.

CHAPTER THREE

The Push-Ahead Woman: When Enough Is Never Enough

I have seen something else under the sun:
The race is not to the swift or the battle to the strong,
nor does food come to the wise
or wealth to the brilliant or favor to the learned;
but time and chance happen to them all.
ECCLESIASTES 9:11

Push-ahead women start out young. In elementary school, our hands probably stabbed the air when the teacher asked for volunteers. When the senior play rolled around, we memorized our own lines, and half the rest for the cast. Our babies were breast-fed, toilet trained, and read to on schedule. Years of reputation were built on our ability to cope, organize, and achieve. That's what being a push-ahead woman is all about.

Most of us probably remember little scenarios and miniature events from our backgrounds where such patterns were set in motion. I remember, in particular, a series of debates in my seventh grade year. In that place, I deepened my conviction that competence and achievement were crucial keys to life.

Over a course of months, these debates became the mental sparring ground around which our class revolved. Week after week, our team won each scheduled debate. But what registered in me was something more than winning. I was discovering that a person's mind could become a useful tool capable of outwitting an opponent through logic and well-chiseled words. I could enter the conceptual, theoretical world I identified as "male" and hold my own.

I was a junior-high version of "I am woman, watch me roar," but being a daughter of the South I knew better than to parade that insight. The lesson was not lost on me, however. The feeling of power and mastery I got from competing well was intoxicating. All the work and race-horse drive seemed to pay off. As the months progressed, my determination to be seen as the "competent woman" on the team grew.

As I grew older, I increasingly relied on my conceptual abilities to unravel whatever knot lay before me. There was a direct connection for me between hard mental work and feeling competent. Even if the applause, the recognition that came from my efforts, was less than deafening, it nevertheless kept me going.

Appearing competent and in control became a hedge against having to deal with what was happening on the inside of me. The illusion was that *as long as I was pushing ahead* I could maintain my equilibrium.

A BRITTLE SHELL WITH A FRAGILE CORE

From all appearances, the lives of push-ahead women usually look great—until you scratch beneath the surface, that is. As long as we can keep all the plates spinning in the air, no one guesses the amount of anxiety and fear that keeps it all in motion. The way we appear—make-up in place, life under control, "do-list" in hand—is often a partial camouflage for the fragile way we feel on the inside.

In reality, in the lives of most women who are given to overdoing there exists something of an outer-inner dichotomy. Though we appear to be successful, "together" individuals, often we feel anything but.

❦

Marie leaned back in her lounge chair and let the sun warm her shoulders as she drifted in and out of the conversation around her. Thursday afternoons in the summer she kept as a protected spot of quiet sanity. Every other day she was either working part-time as an accountant or studying for her CPA exam. Between the laundry, the girls, and cramming for that test, Marie hardly had space to breathe.

From week to week, the group of mothers who came to watch their children swim stayed fairly constant—so did the conversation. Marie called it "female macho" talk. They seemed to vie for first place in who had the fullest calendar, as though an empty space on the schedule was synonymous with the word *lazy*. Like men flexing their muscles, they competed to see who was the busiest. The only difference between Marie and her friends, as far as she could see, was that she was growing a bit weary of it all. Her enthusiasm was at a low ebb.

Marie missed the little things the most—unhurried conversations with her husband, time to read her daughters a book without feeling guilty, the chance to write in her journal. She found herself wondering, at odd moments, if surely there wasn't another way to live.

❦

Like many of us, Marie has a lot going for her. She is smart and capable. Friends marvel at the pace she maintains, the clear goals she sets for herself.

But another word describes her, too: *driven*. Her outward success is marked by a quality of drivenness that is one of the more notable characteristics in the lives of women who can't say no. Marie, herself, is beginning to feel the long-term effects of it.

In their book *We Are Driven*, Doctors Hemfelt, Minirth, and Meier address the issue of "applauded addictions," the compulsive behaviors that our society rewards. Their book is full of examples of people like Marie. Whether it's workaholism or perfectionism or compulsive helping, our culture seems increasingly geared to let such excesses masquerade as virtues. Sometimes only the perceptive person, or those who catch the fallout of drivenness, dare to question the motives beneath the behavior. Then, as Marie did, they wonder if they are the only ones who suspect something is wrong.

These psychologists predict that compulsive behaviors, especially those that are commonly applauded, will reach epidemic proportions in the nineties. They estimate that 75 percent of the people who seek counseling from a pastoral advisor or clinical therapist do so because of an inner sense of drivenness or compulsive behavior they don't know how to stop.[1]

"My friends always used to tell me that they wondered how on earth I kept everything going, but I didn't think my schedule was unusual. I have never known anything else." This comment is often heard from the lips of push-ahead women. They are sincere. A state of constant activity has been a perennial way of life.

I recall sitting on one older woman's front porch and marveling at the view of the Blue Ridge Mountains from her sprawling brick patio. "I bet you really enjoy this," I said to her.

Without skipping a beat, she replied, "I wouldn't know. In the thirty-five years we've lived in this home, I don't recall ever just sitting out here to look at the mountains."

She meant what she said. She had never allowed herself the freedom to prop her feet up for no apparent reason and simply enjoy the panoramic view from her own front porch.

THE MOMENTUM OF DRIVENNESS

It is important to differentiate the drivenness that characterizes the woman who does too much from the saner qualities of faithfulness, attention to detail, and simple hard work. Drivenness is more complicated. It springs from a hotbed of insecurity that makes a person say yes to nearly every opportunity, request, or challenge that comes along. A working definition of drivenness would look something like this: *Drivenness is an overriding compulsion to achieve and accomplish, to stay busy and stay needed by others as a means to gain personal satisfaction and to overcome feelings of shame and inadequacy.*

The driven woman subscribes to a trinity of values: discipline, efficiency, and duty. And she does so without being able to allow much room for balancing virtues like spontaneity and relaxation. Like an acrobat on a tightrope, it appears that only a tightly wired approach will keep life intact.

This is how "doing" takes on a life of its own, one that holds the promise of personal salvation—not in a theological sense, but in a deeply emotional one. The feeling is that if we don't work and work and work to keep everything together, it will all fall apart. In Colette Dowling's book *Perfect Women*, she says that the driven woman believes "accomplishment is what separates the women from the girls. . . . *Doing* makes her feel expansive, powerful."[2] It makes us feel alive.

Plenty of people benefit, directly or indirectly, from the excessive "doing" of the compulsive woman. That's part of what makes drivenness so hard to confront in yourself, or in someone else. Some happy beneficiary will gladly eat the second fresh cherry pie you've fixed or breathe a sigh of relief that you took on that extra report. Your driven behavior is applauded.

As a result, it easily takes on the momentum of any other addiction. This is part of what psychologists call being "addicted to stress." As convoluted as it sounds, the human body so adapts to the high levels of adrenaline that come with living under constant pressure that when a vacation, a day off, or an hour with nothing to do appears, the psychological response is one of agitation. Something feels wrong.

The woman hoping to relax may, in fact, become increasingly anxious, experiencing an ironic discomfort at being peaceful. Consequently, the unconscious tendency is simply to gear up again—and again. Living on the run becomes normal. It took me a long time to realize that my need to throw in a load of laundry when I was running late, comb my hair and put on lipstick at traffic lights, and drop into my foreordained spot in a meeting at the last second was a symptom of how dependent I had become on a busy, frenetic pace. The stress had become as comfortable as an old beanbag chair, positive proof that I had a purpose and place in the scheme of things.

A quality of drivenness comes to characterize the lifestyle of the achieving woman. The strokes and applause she receives for her efforts perform a service: They keep her out of touch with the growing sense of alienation and emptiness in her own heart.

SHALLOW RELATIONSHIPS

Part of what was bothering Marie as she basked in the sun that day was simple loneliness. She knew a wide variety of women, but few, if any, whom she could call *friends.* There were women from her office and church, a handful of other mothers in her neighborhood, but she felt close to none of them really. Most of their conversation consisted of small talk and vacant pleasantries. She felt competent at work, on top of her studying, but relationships were another story. She wasn't sure anymore how to "do" those.

The tendency toward shallow relationships is another observable trait that often characterizes the woman who prizes competence. What others see, as they look on, is a woman who appears untouchable, as though she already has it all together. Relationships don't seem to be high on her priority list, but lack of time and energy are only the symptoms of her problem, not the cause.

It is quite possible, of course, to be a competent person and an intimate friend, someone who is known for personableness as well as expertise. But the woman who consistently works too hard falls into a different category. Her competence is often what *separates* her from real friendship or intimacy. She is too afraid to let her guard down lest someone discover that she is not perfect. Deep down, she is painfully aware that she is only too ordinary. Her competency becomes a barricade against the frightening prospect of being known as she really is.

Others look on from a distance and admire, but not many attempt to scale the fortress. Or, as one brave soul explained to a mutual friend in a particularly honest moment, "I would love to be your friend, Pat. I admire your graphics; you're the epitome of efficiency and artistic perfection. But I feel like I have to earn the privilege to ask you anything personal."

While the achieving woman is left with a growing sense of loneliness, others around her feel the effect of her drivenness. Her own internal pressure to perform spills over into her relationships. Would-be friends and coworkers begin to feel used, like props in someone else's play. I was stunned when a friend admitted to me one day that she often felt the pressure to say something especially insightful when she was with me, as though she had to make it worth my while to spend time with her. I realized that part of the invisible space between us had been created by my own compulsiveness.

The achieving woman often possesses an instinctual ability to impress people. She may be articulate, well-dressed, and well-read, capable of a performance that dazzles. But what she wins is only more admiration, and that eventually feels cheap and undeserved. What she longs for, in reality, is a deeply personal *affirmation* that is only possible when the barricade comes down and another human being is permitted to move in close.

In many ways, the woman who is given to compulsive activity and achievement is in a double bind. All the accolades in the world won't fill the hole in a person's soul, yet those very competencies tend to deflect the help and support that might have come her way. She is in a place of growing isolation and aloneness, of dangling conversations and superficial smiles. Her relational world is symbolized by two hurried acquaintances exchanging polite words. "Gotta run . . . let's do lunch sometime . . . I'll call you."

THE PUSH-AHEAD WOMAN'S INNER WORLD

The woman who does too much is a walking paradox. From all appearances, she lives in a well-ordered, though elusive, world—one that moves forward in syncopated rhythm from one small accomplishment to another. Sure, she may be hard to get to know and a bit driven, but there are privileges that go with her achievements and responsibilities. Those seem to insulate her.

As in so many cases in life, appearances can be

deceiving. The inner dynamics of the overburdened, over-committed woman are a different story—one that is hidden from almost everyone. And for a long time, it can be hidden even from ourselves.

Being on a merry-go-round that is moving too fast is a crazy feeling. An endless string of events and faces run together, and the state of our inner world is far too fragile . . . precariously fragile.

The Inner Void

How is it that outward success can so often be accompanied by an inner sense of self-doubt and emptiness? Perhaps the answer is best explained by the impossible nature of trying to build a true identity on the basis of anything extrinsic to the reality of who we are as women created in the image of God. Let me explain.

Somehow we know, on an unconscious level, that all the "doing" aspects of life have an expiration date stamped on them. Someday we will be too old, too tired, or too matronly to perform. A life centered around what one "does" is a house built on sand, a deck of cards stacked and ready to collapse.

No matter what we accomplished today, or yesterday, if who we are is what we do, then we are only as good as our last success. There will always be a blank computer screen before us, a new class to teach, another load of laundry to sort. If who we are is what we do, then there can be no solid inner place on which to stand.

Besides, women who do too much seem to possess an intractable ability to "discount" their achievements. *"Anybody can wallpaper a bathroom or stencil a wall. It's no big deal, really."* Once I admired the sheer amount of physical work a friend could accomplish in a day, and when I asked her to tell me her secret, she didn't say what I expected. I thought she would smile and tell me how good it felt to have a system that worked as well as hers obviously did. Instead she said, "You know, I grew up on a farm in South Dakota where the work was so endless that whenever someone came to inspect my progress, they felt compelled to point out what was left to be done." In other words, as efficient as this woman was, she felt little inner satisfaction from her work. Like many of us, she saw only the part that was still *undone*. Her successes slid off her like water from a duck's back. They did not stick.

A sense of inner fragility, though, is really born of an unmet need that is deeper than acquiring the ability to count one's achievements significant. It is rooted in the need to capture in the present the recognition and affirmation that were missing in the past. As Colette Dowling wrote,

> Superachievers . . . find themselves in an almost hopeless battle in which they struggle for perfection while at the same time beat themselves down. Lost to them is the child within, the little girl who has always wanted to be admired. They'd be better off by far if they could allow that girl to come forward—if their need for attention could be admitted to, and possibly even met.[3]

Yet that is a need we bury and deny with a vengeance.

Having failed to receive the recognition we longed for as little girls, we spend large portions of our adult lives in search of a suitable substitute. Someday, if we work hard enough, someone will pull us over to the corner of the room, put an arm around our shoulders, look us in the eye, and say, "You are really something. Did you know that?" On some level, that's the hope, anyway.

When that authentic affirmation does not happen—or we can't allow ourselves to receive it—then we tend to come to an unconscious conclusion that is actually the source of our inner precariousness: We conclude that *there is nothing in us worth valuing*; we are not women of substance, women who have something innately valuable to give.

❦

SHORTCHANGED

Marie really liked her boss at work—that was one thing she had going for her. He was a quiet sort of man who ran his firm with precision and skill. He seemed to appreciate Marie's contribution. Enough to let her take a few afternoons off in the summer. Or leave early with no begrudging when one of her daughters was sick.

But Marie could sense that because she was a member of a small firm, her boss was coming to rely heavily on her. The trouble was, she realized, she was almost too good for her own good. When it came to accounting, she was a natural, and her boss knew it.

All of her life Marie had been the kind of person people put in responsible positions. "Always do more than is asked of you. Anticipate what needs to be done, and do it before you're asked"—Marie had absorbed messages like these while growing up, as if someone had sprinkled them on her breakfast cereal every morning. And Marie's hard work had paid off. How many times had someone told her, "I'm giving you this job because I have to have someone I know I can count on"?

It was a strange feeling for Marie to reach a point where she wanted to wave a white flag and yell,

---

"Stop! No more!" She hated the thought of disappointing her boss by asking him to relieve her of
some of the load she was carrying. In some ways,
Marie realized that her competence had programed
him to think of her as Wonder Woman. She had set
herself up. The better she did at her job, the more
work she was given to do.

Here she was, within months of passing the big
exam, yet it seemed that if the "prize" meant a life
filled with more of the same, then she must be winning some sort of booby prize.

❦

A note of betrayal and disappointment, like the one you
hear in Marie's story, is a common part of the interior
world of women who are known for doing.

When what you achieve is, in some intrinsic way,
necessary to validate your life, then it is inevitable that
reaching a goal will feel like pouring water through a sieve.
We can't help but feel shortchanged. "I worked this hard
for *this*?! This is it?" The glow wears off so quickly, and
there we are, pretty much the same women we were all
along—which was precisely the problem to begin with.

Authors Hardesty and Jacobs interviewed women
in the business world who had given large chunks of
their lives to climbing someone's corporate ladder. They
found that this theme of "success and betrayal" was a
common thread in many women's stories. "The sense
of betrayal sneaks up on so many women," they wrote.
The public sees "only the mastery, never the misery."[4]
For women who succumb to the unconscious tendency
to marry their job and make the workplace their family—looking for caring, recognition, and acceptance in

the process—the disappointment is even greater. There, recognition comes in the form of more responsibility and more money, both of which wear thin in the long run. Often, in this sense, "women lose *especially* when they win."[5]

The lives of women who tend to be over-responsible and over-achieving are often characterized by a free-floating anger. One friend described the feeling of being "held hostage." Unaware of the internal demand that kept her racing through her days, all she could see was that the better she performed, the more dependent she became financially on the lifestyle her income afforded her. She described the feeling in poignant words. "I'm going nowhere, it seems, but I'm getting there very quickly."

The feeling of being shortchanged can be present even for the woman who has poured her energy into home and family. Children have a strange way of resisting expectations. They can turn their backs on years of nurturing and head in the opposite direction. Sometimes the "investment" doesn't pay the hoped-for dividends, and all our effort appears to be for naught.

Repulsed by the Thought of Weakness

I have a friend, a research chemist, who often works on assigned projects as a member of a small task force. She found herself in a tight spot recently when, after working nonstop toward a pressing deadline, she felt the onset of flu. She knew from her medical history that she should quietly excuse herself and go home.

Instead she toughed it out. Without mentioning that she was sick, she worked until the project was finished, left with a 102 degree temperature, and spent the next week in bed recovering. I asked her why. Why didn't she just say she wasn't feeling well?

"I hated to admit that I wasn't holding up under the strain," she replied.

✗me The tough girl, I-can-handle-it mode of living—a common response of the push-ahead woman—is, in actuality, a reaction against anything that appears weak. And unfortunately, whatever seems "feminine" is often seen as "weakness."[6] By feminine, I mean in this case the softer parts of our personality, our natural needs for help and support, our longings to be cared for and protected. These healthy desires get mislabeled and lumped in the emotional category of "weakness," and thereby rejected.

From this void, then, we tend to gravitate in the direction of a false version of strength, one most often caricatured in masculine overtones (as it was for me in my debating experience). "Strength" in this sense is equated with power and mastery. The lure of this kind of strength is that it provides the illusion of calling the shots, of coming out on top, of being in control.

What is beneath our fear of giving up control? Dr. Toni Grant, in her book *Being a Woman*, says that for many women "giving up control often uncovers a profound fear of dependency and vulnerability."[7] These denote "weakness" from which we resolutely stay away.

Not only do we mislabel our definition of weakness, though. In the process, we often lose touch with our true feminine strengths. Perhaps those strengths could be best expressed in that wide repertoire of relational abilities by which we make personal an impersonal world—our receptivity and responsiveness, the "involvement and attachment and invitation [that] belong more clearly to the feminine identity."[8]

The push-ahead woman too often ends up viewing the vulnerable aspects of being a woman as a handicap to overcome. Relying on anyone besides herself begins to seem like a luxury she can ill afford. And her emotional life winds down tighter and tighter under the rigid confines of maintaining control.

In the next chapter, we will explore another way that

we overextend ourselves as women. The indispensable woman has her own particular way of overdoing it. And she, too, pays an enormous price.

NOTES
1. Drs. Hemfelt, Minirth, and Meier, *We Are Driven* (Nashville: Thomas Nelson, 1991), page 8.
2. Colette Dowling, *Perfect Women* (New York: Simon & Schuster, 1988), page 73.
3. Dowling, page 80.
4. Sarah Hardesty and Nehama Jacobs, *Success and Betrayal* (New York: Franklin Watts, 1986), page 20.
5. Hardesty and Jacobs, page 54.
6. Dr. Toni Grant, *Being a Woman* (New York: Avon Books, 1988), page 7.
7. Grant, page 76.
8. Dr. Larry Crabb, *Men and Women: Enjoying the Difference* (Grand Rapids: Zondervan, 1991), pages 161-162.

CHAPTER FOUR

The Indispensable Woman: When You Give Until It Hurts

Martha was distracted by all the preparations that had to be made. She came to him and asked, "Lord, don't you care that my sister has left me to do the work by myself? Tell her to help me!"
LUKE 10:40

Julie breathed an audible sigh of relief when some-one else moved to adjourn the meeting. *Good,* she thought, *maybe I'll get home in time to make sure the kids get to bed at a decent hour.*

Just as she was ready to make a dash for the door, though, her friend caught her eye. Julie was the kind of woman to whom others readily told their troubles. She'd known Maggie only a short while before Maggie's marital difficulties became the common topic of conversation.

"Could I talk with you for a minute?" Maggie asked.

Julie could tell by her expression that whatever was bothering her was more than a minute's worth. But, then, what do you say? "Sure," Julie responded, and for the next hour her friend poured out her story, while Julie stifled the urge to glance at her watch.

As she drove home, Julie tried rehearsing more acceptable ways to exit a conversation like the one she had just finished. This was not an isolated incident—it was a lifelong pattern. She could be bone tired, running with her tongue hanging out, but just show her someone with a need, a big need, and she was drawn like a magnet. Just the other day her husband had looked at her and said, "Honey, why do you feel compelled to become the den mother for every group you are a part of? It's killing you."

Julie was now on her third reading of the same time-management book, but she felt no closer to a sane schedule. She knew she needed to cut back, and goodness knows she had tried. Her calendar was color-coded, planned well in advance. But it usually took only a friend's or child's disappointment or need of her to trigger such hyper-responsibility that she went on automatic pilot. Forget the schedule.

Lately, though, she had been so irritable and tired, she actually found herself plotting ways to avoid people. She felt like a cow without enough udders. A nagging question had begun to form in the back of her mind: *Why is it,* she wondered, *that I always seem to be on the giving end? Why do so few people ever ask how I'm doing?*

❦

Julie is an indispensable woman. If you recognize her as one of your friends—or if she's you—then you quickly realize that some fine qualities get this woman into trouble.

Warm, caring, outgoing, immensely likable—the indispensable woman is equipped with a set of finely tuned antennae that enable her to detect a need and move toward meeting it before most people are aware of its existence. A downcast glance or a furrowed eyebrow, a tiny tremor in someone's lower lip—she's not always sure how she perceives another person's hurt, she just *knows*. In fact, her people skills are so multifaceted, her propensity for giving to others is so consistent, that in many circles she is the model others seek to emulate.

She has such admirable qualities that it often takes years before she—or anyone else in her life, for that matter—questions what her giving is all about. Do you need a letter typed or an errand run? Has no one offered to organize this year's walk-a-thon? The indispensable woman will rise to the occasion. Even when she thinks "no," it seems to come out "yes." She has learned to make her life work by filling in the gaps of everyone else's. And no one complains very quickly about a situation where the "problem" appears to be only that your needs are too well met.

Yet there is a problem. And way down deep, the indispensable woman senses something is amiss. She struggles for limits and boundaries, for someone who will lift this enormous, undefinable load off her back.

Like Julie, she eventually grows weary of being everyone's confidante. It's too much of a good thing, as the old saying goes. She is stuck on a treadmill that is going in only one direction. As one indispensable friend, a pastor's wife, admitted in a moment of honesty, "The ministry seems to be full of one-way relationships. Is that the way it's supposed to be?" She was beginning to sense the abject loneliness behind that feeling of always being on the giving end.

The compulsive tendencies of the indispensable woman, as virtuous as they appear, can be balanced only by looking more closely at what lies beneath them. A deeper understanding of her drive to do too much reveals false beliefs and hidden emotions that fuel the intensity of the way she lives. The questions that lead her beneath the surface of her life are many. Why, for instance, does she continue to extend herself way beyond reasonable limits, often when her efforts are not even in another person's best interests?

Why does she give until it hurts?

THE INDISPENSABLE WOMAN'S CORE BELIEFS

You may look at Julie's story, or the life of another indispensable woman, and initially mistake her for the woman we discussed in the previous chapter: the push-ahead woman, whose obsessions center around issues of competence. It's true that the indispensable woman can be as driven as the next woman. Her relationships often lack depth and meaning. She is no stranger to efficiency and hard work.

But a different twist to her story is worthy of noting. The focus of the indispensable woman's overdoing is *people*—not projects or clear-cut goals that measure progress in a particular direction. She is the maypole around which others dance. Some deep ache in her is seeking to be soothed while she is busy meeting other people's needs. She lives to please, while the push-ahead woman strives to achieve.

If you looked inside her mind and tried to understand the notions that propel her into a lifestyle of giving until it hurts, you would discover that, underneath it all, two beliefs form the core of her overdoing.

Like most inner convictions, the strength of these beliefs' hold on us lies in the fact that they are buried so deep we are not consciously aware of their existence. It's only after we are well down the road in our own journey that we may be able to own their presence. *"Oh, yeah, now I see that is indeed the way I've looked at life, and now I understand why."* Owning the inner statements that have motivated us is a fundamental part of changing those patterns.

My Purpose in Life Is to Meet Other People's Needs
In 1987, Miles Laboratory set out to study the sources of stress in women's lives, and they isolated that stress by geographical regions. Women in the south came in second (which I noted with no surprise). But listen to the reason these women gave for the pressure they felt: Six out of ten said they experienced high levels of stress because they felt compelled to meet everyone's needs and demands on their time and energies. Most said that they put themselves last when it came to getting needs met.

In reality, there is a little bit of "southern woman" in each of us, I suspect. We know what it's like to feel torn between a committee meeting and a friend's crisis, between longing to read the paper in peace and little voices calling "Mom!" Responsiveness is part of our nature, a special "attuned-ness" God builds into our make-up.

For the indispensable woman, though, the ability to respond to others' needs gets stuck in overdrive. *She takes her capacity to meet needs and builds her identity around it.*

Sue Monk Kidd, in her book about the inner passages of women, wrote, "I sometimes felt that I had been scripted to be all things to all people."[1] She called that playing the role of the good little girl. Like an orchid in a hothouse, she was fragile, pleasing, pressed between the pages of someone else's scrapbook. She was someone's mother, someone's wife, someone's Sunday school teacher, someone's employee. Put there to meet whatever the need was, she was an amorphous glob of putty that, supposedly, could take on any shape the situation called for. It's just that deep down, on a soul level, the question is still left nagging, "Who am I?"

Finding your own identity in pleasing other people and meeting their needs appears, at least on the surface, to provide a justifiable purpose to life. For many of us, one way we internalize this belief is by becoming a conductor, a bridge in others' relationships. Often, we have functioned in that capacity since we were quite small.

One bright, attractive woman, a high school teacher who struggles with depression, explained how as a little girl she had been the go-between in her parents' arguments. When they were angry, they could go for as long as two weeks at a time without talking to each other directly.

"Rachel," her dad would say, "tell your mother that I won't be home for dinner."

"Well, you tell him to go by the bank before it closes today," her mother would funnel back through Rachel.

What about Rachel? Like anyone who gets caught as the traffic controller in someone else's relationship, she had a mixture of reactions, even as a child. On one hand, she felt that in some strange way, she was important. Here she was as a six-year-old conducting significant business between two adults. She *mattered* – or at least it seemed as if she did. What a sense of power, especially for a child, to be one side of the triangle in a relationship with adults.

But there is another side to being that kind of relational bridge. The one time that Rachel could be sure of her parents' rapt attention was when she was the connection between the two of them. This is one major way that she learned the role of being an indispensable woman. Her identity was forged around the task of figuring out what someone needed and providing it the best way she could. Her purpose in life was intimately connected to a service she performed for others.

This is just one example of how we learn, early on, that our relational abilities can provide us with an intoxicating sense of being needed. What comes through, though, is that our services are desirable – not *us*. The function we provide for someone else becomes our reason for being. We feel wanted by others, necessary to make their lives go more smoothly. *Indispensable* is the word.

Everything Depends on Me

This second inner belief is an especially hard one for the indispensable woman to acknowledge. The crisis or need she is trying to meet looms so large that her own over-responsible role as rescuer and caretaker appears small in comparison. But the way she lives gives her inner conviction away: *If I'm not there to hold the situation together, it will surely fall apart.* And often, simply because her family and friends are trained to rely on her as superwoman, if she does downscale her contribution, things may indeed feel rather wobbly.

The indispensable woman gives the impression of being strong and capable, an independent soul who can stand on her own two feet. She is the one to whom others turn in their time of distress.

Listen to the way one indispensable woman, a counselor in her mid-forties, describes herself: "All my adult life as a single woman I had perceived myself to be a rather strong, independent go-getter. Rarely asking help with anything, I was committed not to bother people, not to be in anyone's debt. If something broke, I either fixed it myself or paid someone else to do it. I changed my own oil, fixed my own flat tires, handled the closing on my first home, and dug my own hole when I wanted to plant a tree. I was always in charge. Most often, I was the one to say, 'Don't worry, we'll take my car, or 'I've got money, so I'll pick up the food.' To allow anyone to inconvenience himself for me seemed the height of presumption."[2]

The notion that "everything depends on me" usually gets deeply embedded in the heart of an indispensable woman during an early crisis time in her life. There, indeed, through a child's eyes, it appeared that she was the only one who could come to the rescue. Something crucial was at stake.

A friend remembers how absolutely incapacitated her alcoholic mother was when her father finally moved to a place of his own. At night she would listen to her mother cry in her bedroom, and before long, she would tiptoe in and climb in bed with her. She remembers falling asleep, night after night, with her arms around her mother's neck, as though it was her comfort and presence that gave them both sleep. The message that she internalized was simple: *If mother and I are going to survive, I will have to come to the rescue. This situation depends on me.*

As an adult, my friend finds it hard to give up responsibility in any given situation. The fear of impending doom is enormous. Somehow if she's not right there holding the roof up, so to speak, it will all cave in.

When we see our purpose in life as fused with our ability to help others, when the responsibility somehow rests on us, we inevitably come to carry a load that is far bigger than our shoulders were meant to carry. We take on burdens and responsibilities that rightfully belong to others. Or if we leave them where they belong, we battle false guilt as though someone might accuse us, at any moment, of loafing on the job.

While some people sort through who should do what as easily as they separate a load of laundry to wash, to the indispensable woman, it's all one big pile. She has little idea where another person's responsibilities stop and hers begin.

In the sixth chapter of Galatians, the Apostle Paul talks about the necessity of each person carrying his or her own load in life (Galatians 6:5). The Greek word for load in this passage is the equivalent of *knapsack*.[3] Each person is to carry her own knapsack. The daily essentials of life—her opinions and feelings, her use of time and money, the repercussions of the choices she makes—are the supplies that go in each person's backpack.

We are responsible to carry our own load in life. The symbolic dilemma of the indispensable woman is that she carries her own knapsack—as well as the knapsack of those who are unwilling or too tired to carry their own. In the process, she grows bent under a load she was never meant to bear, while others get a free ride and circumvent the growth and challenge they truly need.

HIDDEN EMOTIONS: ANGER AND FEAR

One afternoon, not long after we moved to North Carolina, I found myself in the thick of an impossible situation. On the surface it was absolutely comical. I might have laughed, except that it struck me as a living metaphor for my own brand of "indispensability."

My husband was out of town. And I had decided that this was the weekend to show our two children and my aging parents the sights and wonders of the greater Raleigh area. Never mind that I was new to the city and not skilled at reading a map. We headed for the botanical gardens so my parents could admire the roses, but it rained. I plied the kids with intermittent playgrounds and the privilege of riding in the back seat of the station wagon on a trip they grew tired of after an hour. I tried hard to keep everybody happy.

Finally, after wandering back roads not shown on any map, we pulled into a restaurant for lunch—right before they switched to the dinner menu. There at the table it all came to a head. On one side of me sat my elderly father, in sore need of a hearing aid, repeatedly saying, "Talk louder, I can't hear you," while my daughter sat on my other side, tugging at my skirt and pleading for a dollar to buy a giant jawbreaker! I felt like a piece of saltwater taffy.

My first impulse was to laugh at the absurdity of the situation, but the humor was short-lived. I had spent too much of my life in this manner—torn in five directions at once, flitting from one person's expectation to the next, trying too hard to keep everything smooth and everybody happy. Even though I "minor" in being an indis-

pensable woman as my chosen means of overdoing, still
the tendency is strong enough to wreak sufficient havoc
in my life.

I have lived this way enough to understand that feeling of being fragmented, as though (in T. S. Eliot's words)
I had "measured out my life in coffee spoons." Isn't that
a descriptive phrase? Measuring out your life in coffee
spoons is the feeling of being fragmented. A little here, a
little there, until it seems there is nothing left.

I understand the feeling of being gobbled up, inhaled
by the depth of the needs around you. And I recognize
that beneath the powerlessness of feeling at everyone's
disposal there exists enough subterranean anger to tilt
the planet off its axis.

Anger

No aspect of your world as an indispensable woman is
harder to pinpoint and address than your anger. For admitting you were angry because others did not readily relate
to you as hoped would be to admit that you had needs
yourself. That you couldn't make it on your own. Anger is
not a pretty word. It stands in stark contrast to the model
woman who is always giving, so selflessly, it seems, never
asking for help or comfort in return.

Yet hidden anger stalks our lives when our penchant
is compulsive doing for others. Here is how Nancy Friday
described indispensable women and our hard-to-admit
anger in her book *My Mother/My Self*:

> The compulsive housekeeper, the lioness of Anti-
> Porn Society, the nonstop charity-worker, the
> overprotective and critical mother who does it all for
> someone else's good—who can fault these people
> out loud? . . . Very often, these women are obses-
> sive/compulsives—suffering from forms of behavior
> that seem to have nothing to do with anger. Unlike

depressed people who turn their anger within, against themselves, *the obsessive/compulsives express theirs outwardly—but in such an indirect way they never need face their furies at all.*[4] (emphasis added)

Indispensable women have a whole repertoire of ways to keep from walking directly into our frustration and anger. As in the impossible day in my own life I just related, we shrug them off and chuckle them away. "What a crazy life I lead," we say and keep on smiling. We take our frustration and bury it, rather than admit that maybe fatigue and hunger and needing someone else's help are also parts of being human.

What happens to the indispensable woman who, like the bunny with the EverReady battery, somehow manages to keep going and going and going? What happens to the woman who never faces her anger over being forever stuck on the giving end?

She hardens quietly on the inside into the self-imposed prison of the proverbial female martyr. If being angry is not a pretty picture, martyrdom is less still. But that's where anger, when left unacknowledged, leads.

I have a picture in my mind of a female martyr. I'm convinced there is at least one woman like this in every family. She might be your grandmother or a little old aunt. As long as there is breath in her body, she will be the first to rise from the holiday table and carry dishes to the sink. Everyone else is just about ready to relax and savor their coffee, but Aunt Martha is already running water in the kitchen. One by one most of the women slowly follow suit. It would be terrible to let Martha do all that work alone. She is so frozen in her over-productivity that other women feel under-productive in her presence. They wish they had the nerve to say, "The dishes can wait, Martha. Sit down, and let us visit with *you*."

Can you sense the set-in-cement anger in Aunt Martha's trek to the kitchen? Can you feel the fear that maybe, just maybe, if she stays at the table she will start to feel her sister's cold shoulder? Or maybe someone will discover that she doesn't have that much to say, that she will seem ordinary, inadequate, as bland as an ungarnished baked potato. The martyr is an angry woman who never lets herself stop long enough to feel her own feelings and let them direct her to the sources of pain or discomfort.

Facing your anger as an indispensable woman is difficult to do because it leads to some rather obvious questions: Why haven't you asked for someone's help, long before now? Why haven't you held off until someone else finally picks up their share of the load? Why don't you just simply leave the job undone, the need unmet?

Why, in the words of Olivia Newton John, have you never let someone else be strong?

ॐ

The Underlying Fear
Julie unlocked her front door and quietly tiptoed into the darkened living room. *Good,* she thought to herself, *it looks as if everyone's in bed.* She poured herself a cup of leftover decaf, then sank into one corner of her overstuffed sofa.

When she first became aware of her husband's presence, he was standing right next to her. She sat up with a jolt. "Where did you come from?" she asked, as she motioned for Steve to take a seat beside her. "I didn't hear you at all."

"Where have *you* been? I've been waiting up for you," Steve said. Julie tried to ignore the little gleam in his eye. "Tell me about your meeting," he prodded.

From there Julie drew him a verbal picture of the events and people in her evening. Steve groaned at the indecision of the PTA committee. Since Christmas, they had been stalled between two different sets of playground equipment. And he sympathized with Julie's effort to give sane advice to a friend whose husband was threatening to seek custody of their children.

"You know, honey, you can't solve all those problems tonight," Steve finally said. He put his arm around her and began to nibble playfully on her earlobe.

Julie knew where this was heading. Mentally, she began to pull herself away from her meeting and her friend's problems and turn her attention to this moment. She put down her coffee cup and returned Steve's embrace. Inwardly, though, she stifled a groan.

Sometimes it felt like she was just a pie—and everyone wanted a piece.

❦

It is in private moments, such as this one between Julie and Steve, that the interpersonal dilemma of the indispensable woman can be most clearly seen. For what Steve is asking of Julie in this late night exchange is, in actuality, a sharing of *herself*. Any kind of true connection between people—especially genuine physical intimacy—requires that we be present inside our own body so that we can give ourselves to the person we love. That kind of giving is something like having an internal doorknob, one that we can reach and turn and thereby invite another person into the true place we inhabit.

But for Julie, physical intimacy is really another exercise in meeting someone's needs. It represents yet another person's tank to fill. For her, sex is not a time of respite from a pressured day, a chance to connect with the person on the planet to whom she is closest. It is more a necessary chore. While Julie hardly ever turns her husband down, she sometimes wonders why he rarely seems really satisfied. "Where are *you* in this, honey?" he asks occasionally. What Julie does not see is that, even in her giving, she is depriving Steve of what he longs for most: her honest, unabashed desire for him.

Her own desires and wants and needs—these are what are missing from the picture of Julie's life, or the life of any other indispensable woman. She locked these needs and desires in a dark closet long ago, a closet that is labeled "selfish" or "ugly."

I once asked a friend who was trying to decide which direction to head now that her children were in school, a friend known for her indispensability, what she *wanted* to do. What did she enjoy? Her face went totally blank. "Enjoy?" she said. "The question of what I just plain *want* to do has never been a category in my thinking."

Yet our needs and desires are integral parts of being human, of being women made in the image of God. As the psalmist cried, "Lord, all my *desire* is before Thee; and my sighing is not hidden from Thee" (Psalm 38:9, NASB, emphasis added). Our desires and needs form the passion that keeps us returning to God as the One who satisfies a longing heart. And they are also part of the glue that makes any relationship a real relationship. It is my honest desire or need of my husband, for example, that makes me truly want to enjoy a cup of coffee with him or hug his neck—or even wring his neck! The recognition of my own needs and desires enables me to be present with him.

When a woman is out of touch with what she wants or needs, her giving seems hollow to others. It's as if they had been visited by Tinkerbell, who flits about but never lights long enough for anyone to touch her or be truly touched by her. In the true sense of the word, the indispensable woman is guilty of *selfless* giving—literally giving without a self. That is why, even though her giving can appear quite caring, it often feels superficial to the recipient. The indispensable woman has yet to realize that her own need might be something of a gift to another human being, an invitation to a genuine reciprocal relationship.

The woman who has built her life around helping others feels a great sense of humiliation when her own neediness is exposed. She finds it difficult to ask for help or comfort for herself. As one woman explained, "Eventually I had to agree that giving had been safer for me than receiving, and I had chosen to surround myself with lots of needy people because it was less threatening than exposing my own need for compassion . . . *to be known as needy shamed me*"[5] (emphasis added).

So the indispensable woman concocts a superhuman image of herself rather than face her own insecurities. She finds a way to remain the strong one in relationships, the one who gives and never needs. The giving side of herself she casts in virtuous tones; her needy, longing parts she disowns. Another woman wrote, "A 'spiritual' woman (my goal in life) didn't need others, I thought; her task was to give, not take. When I finally acknowledged I *did* have needs like everyone else, I had to get off my pedestal and welcome myself to the human race. The shame was awful. So was the fear."[6]

What, more precisely, is the fear at the root of the indispensable woman's tendency to overdo? It is more than the fear that if her real needs and desires become known, they may go unmet. What strikes a deeper terror to her soul—and the reason she must make herself indispensable in others' lives—is the fear that if she doesn't, she will be left all alone, either literally or emotionally. Only her usefulness seems to guarantee her a central place in someone's life. She sees herself as a "blank slate," sitting vacant, waiting for someone else's expectation or need to give her definition.

The fear is that there is nothing inherently lovable or desirable in her that would cause others to want a relationship with her totally apart from the useful functions she performs. Considering her own wants and needs, her dreams and desires, causes her to take a look inside. And her great fear, when she looks inside, is that she or others will discover *there is no one home.*

She must make herself indispensable in order to gain some assurance that she is wanted by others.

This, then, is the predicament of those of us whose version of doing too much centers around keeping the people in our lives pleased and happy and fixed. The challenge before us is to face what's happening inside us—our honest thoughts and feelings as we relate to others. As we do that, we are likely to encounter a pendulum swing of highs and lows, a common cycle of hope and despair that keeps our overdoing stuck in overdrive. This is the subject of the next chapter.

NOTES
1. Sue Monk Kidd, *When the Heart Waits* (San Francisco: Harper & Row, 1990), page 6.
2. Lottie Hillard, "Overcoming the Shame of Needing," *IBC Perspective,* page 9.
3. Dr. John Townsend, *Hiding from Love* (Colorado Springs: NavPress, 1991), page 78.
4. As quoted in Sandra Simpson LeSourd, *The Compulsive Woman* (Old Tappan: Fleming H. Revell Co., 1987), page 61.
5. Hillard, page 10.
6. Nancy Groom, *From Bondage to Bonding* (Colorado Springs: NavPress, 1991), page 5.

CHAPTER FIVE

Ecstasy and Agony:
As the Pendulum Swings

For by the grace given me I say to every one of you:
Do not think of yourself more highly than you ought,
but rather think of yourself with sober judgment,
in accordance with the measure of faith
God has given you.
ROMANS 12:3

"Do you think you can handle a trip like this alone?" my husband asked, as he watched me finish packing my suitcase. The tone of doubt in his voice was obvious. "You know, you don't *have* to go to Dallas this summer. It can wait."

Somewhere in my head, I heard his words and I knew he was right. But a trip to Texas to visit fifty families from the church that supported our ministry was two years overdue. I knew that, too. At the last minute, when Stacy's services had been needed to run a conference center for the summer, I volunteered to take our two children and make this three-week trip in his place.

I had great intentions. The strategy was all mapped out in my mind. Some couples I would invite to dinner; others I would meet for lunch. A metropolitan map of the entire area held pinpricks where I planned to visit people who had moved to surrounding suburbs. It would be a challenge, I knew, to visit fifty families in three weeks, but then that was part of what appealed to me. If it was a *big* challenge, then at the end of the trip I would feel as though I had accomplished something significant.

Needless to say, I had not factored children with strep throats and infected bee stings into my plans. Nor had I been honest about how tired I was, even going into the trip. I had forgotten, as well, what it was like to be caught in six lanes of rush hour traffic with two children as you tried to decide which exit to take. "Oh, Lord," I remember praying, "if You will just get us off this road in one piece, I will never get out here at this time of day again, I promise."

By the end of the trip, I had seen most of the people I came to Dallas to see. The challenge had been met, but I was really tired now. My eyes brimmed with tears over small things.

I knew I had reached a new level of fatigue when, after volunteering to take a friend and her children to the zoo, I realized I could not make the return trip without a nap. I would fall asleep while driving, as tired as I felt.

Rather than ask my friend to drive, rather than admit my fatigue, I asked instead for a few minutes to "freshen up." I disappeared around the corner and headed straight for the ladies' room. All my life I have been known for my ability to take naps in strange places, at strange times. Never before, though, had I been desperate enough to find a stall in a public restroom, lock the door, take a seat on the toilet, fully clothed, and fall soundly asleep with my head propped against the wall for fifteen minutes.

When I awoke, I was still tired but I knew I could make it home. By the time my friend saw me, I had put on fresh lipstick and a smile.

❧

The summer scenario I have just described took place about five years ago, before I understood very much about the inner dynamics of my life. It is a classic snapshot of a woman who is caught on an invisible treadmill — one of her own making, in many ways — an endless cycle of ups and downs, of forging ahead in moments that actually call for quite another response.

This cycle is known by an off-putting phrase called "grandiosity and shame."[1] This describes the pair of extremes that are operative in a woman whose life is dominated by the drive to do too much. For in truth, she spends much of her life straddled between two emotional poles: feeling on some days that she can take on the world; while on others, she doubts her ability to walk around the block. Small wonder she sometimes describes herself as "strung out." She swings between shame and "grandiosity," which is the sense of being, or needing to be, *more* than she humanly is to protect herself from the downside of that cycle — feeling irredeemably less. It's like overinflating a tire and watching it pop, time and time again, because it would not be enough simply to ride on the tire as it is.

When you consider my story, you can see all the basic elements of this cycle in place. Wouldn't it be wonderful if I could haul two kids around a metropolis like Dallas and visit all those folks myself?! Other women might not be able to pull off such a feat. But then, I never wanted to think of myself as an ordinary woman. Such a trip would call for superior planning and forethought, for the public relations ability of a goodwill ambassador. The sheer difficulty challenged me. *If it's a good cause and I work hard enough, I can do almost anything.* These are the subtle, unconscious mental underpinnings of a woman who needs to feel superhuman.

The downside of my story is just as evident. No one forced me to make the trip in the first place. I could have said no. Or I could have made the trip and settled for limited objectives, living at a saner pace during those weeks. There was freedom to accept the limits of my mortality at any point. What kept me from taking any of these options was a hesitancy inside of me. It seemed embarrassing—shameful—to admit aloud that I was an ordinary human being, a woman too tired even to make the drive home.

THE NEED TO FEEL LIKE MORE

Where does this cycle of grandiosity and shame come from? In many ways, it is rooted in our innate longing for perfection. We are no longer living in the paradise we were created for, but we have not lost our instinctive memory of the kind of perfection the Garden of Eden represents. We aim "high" because we carry around in our minds an innate sense of how things ought to be. This is our lost recollection of paradise, an internal barometer of perfection.

The perfection we lost when sin first came into that garden cannot be retrieved, though, no matter how hard we try. The harder we aim for the ideal on our own effort and steam, the more we bounce between elation when it appears we are nearing our "goal" and despair when it becomes apparent we are not. The only way out is to accept our human limitations and turn our humble hearts toward the worship of One who is truly perfect.

In a spiritual sense, the phenomenon of grandiosity is not unlike Isaiah's description of Lucifer's attitude toward his place in creation. Not content to be the angel, the "morning star" he was created to be, he insisted on being more: "I will ascend to heaven; I will raise my throne above the stars of God" (Isaiah 14:13). Five times he uses the phrase, "I will" as though his place in the scheme of things were something of his own choosing. As though perfection, or life as he envisioned it, was within his reach. Simply being an angel was not enough.

The seed of this same willful autonomy resonates

within the deep-set convictions of those given to over-doing. Our striving is evidence of a determination to be our own strength. There is pressure in the notion that it will all fall apart without us, but there is also a lot of pride.

It is as though, in our minds, the woman God made each of us to be is declared not enough. Rather than embracing our humanity and incompleteness as our true route to dependence on God, we determine to transcend those limitations. We kick against goads and set about weaving together our own fig leaves to cover our nakedness.[2]

> "I must be the brightest, the best." ✳
> "I will make this situation work out right." ✳
> "I have to be the strong one because no one else will." ✳
> "I will find some way to make this person pay attention to me."

Grandiosity, or the need to be more than who you are to keep from feeling like less, evidences itself in at least two subtle, but pernicious ways.

Inflated Notions
On the up-side of this cycle, the woman who can't say no sees herself and her life as if neither held any inherent limitations. It seems as though she can do almost anything if she just tries hard enough. She has something for everyone.

It's like having a moving mirage posted out in front of you that exerts an irresistible pull. The illusion is that if you take on one more project or satisfy the expectations of one more person, then maybe you can coast awhile. Of course, that moment to relax never comes. The next mirage has already materialized to take the place of the last one. Only by more achievement, more work can you keep the larger-than-life feeling, which in its best moments is close to euphoria. "As far back as I can remember," one woman explained, "I have wanted to be more. Regardless of how I'm doing or what anyone says, I yearn to be better, prettier, smarter."[3]

The Need to Be Special
Everyone needs to feel special, as though they matter to God and to others. The compulsive person, though, needs to feel *special* to feel like anyone at all. Being admired and being loved are almost one and the same thing. Whatever the cost, she must keep the applause coming. She is always on the lookout for that "one moment in time" when she becomes more than she thought she could be.

Being ordinary or average—being just one among many—is tantamount to failure, because such an admission forces her to let go of the feeling of being special. She performs for other people's attention by being the "best" in school or on the job, the most popular, the thinnest. Only by being phenomenal can she be sure that she exists.

The excess in the drive and compulsion of the woman who does too much is actually an overreaction to feelings that begin in childhood. "Nothing I have done or been or received has been enough"—this is the little girl's experience of life. As Colette Dowling wrote in *Perfect Women*, "So she compensates. . . . What she feels is left out, as if something is missing. Her feelings of deprivation turn into an 'I'll get mine' compulsion that pumps up and down in her like pistons driving an engine."[4] She *will* be the best, the brightest, the most helpful—or she will bust her engine trying. And someday, maybe, she will do something grand enough to be welcomed with open arms.

In adulthood, she gets caught between a rock and a hard place. *She is forever trying to improve herself—yet she longs to be accepted just as she is.*[5] In one sense, she is a

unconditional love.

Excellent

plain, homely little girl who wants only to be recognized; yet there is also inside of her an exquisite ballerina who longs to dazzle her audience and shine in an iridescent glow. She is caught between the two, needing to see both the plain little girl and the beautiful ballerina as one who has been embraced in the loving arms of a true Father who does not require that she perform.

Perhaps one of the saddest aspects of the cycle between grandiosity and shame is that it sets us up for perennial disillusionment. When our most cherished ideal is perfection, then almost everything else seems vaguely disappointing.

We move through life enticed and tantalized by empty hopes, placing our faith in people and achievements that seem to offer what only God has promised to give. C.S. Lewis used a particular phrase to describe this kind of deception. He called it "*the sweet poison of a false infinite.*"[6] In insisting on perfection in the form of being the best, the brightest, the most spiritual, the prettiest, we serve false gods. And such gods always break the hearts of those who worship them. The inner torment in chasing the false ideal of perfection is that it remains forever beyond our reach—and the chase itself leaves us only progressively more empty.

excellent

It is as though we have a hole in our soul—and all our efforts to fill that hole only make it larger.

❦

TO KEEP FROM FEELING LESS

As long as Kay could find a stage to sing on, she was fine. Unlike most people, she felt comfortable in a spotlight. She had sung her way through a myriad of beauty pageants and singing contests growing up. Pink taffeta gowns, music scores, and the proud glow of her mother's eyes in the audience—these were things Kay associated with the world of music. On stage, she was at her best.

It's just that now, with three small children, Kay had reached a point in her life where she had neither the time nor the opportunity to keep her music as central as it had been in the past.

Making beds and cooking meals, playing "ride a little horsey" on the floor with her children—Kay saw her days passing by in a blur of activities, none of which were her forte, really. Growing up, she had been so busy with school and singing that she never learned basic household tasks. It was her sister, everyone agreed, who was the "domestic" one. Kay lived to sing.

Now that she was married and had her own home, she managed to get her act together when friends came for dinner. There were two or three "company meals" she could prepare—just enough to keep anyone from guessing how inept she felt when it came to caring for a home and a family. She was okay, that is, until her mother-in-law came on one of her regular visits.

Her husband's mother was the original Betty Crocker homemaker. If Kay didn't find ways to occupy her, Mrs. Brown would follow her around the house all day—straightening up little messes, showing her how to organize the spice cabinet. Kay knew she meant well. But knowing those good intentions did nothing to untie the knot in her stomach whenever she saw her mother-in-law's suitcase on the inside of her front door. Every cluttered room, every unwiped nose held damning evidence. Before long, her mother-in-law would have even more proof of

> what Kay had always feared was true: she didn't
> have what it took to be a real wife and mother—to be
> a real woman.

In Kay's life we see what happens on the down-side of the
grandiosity-shame cycle. A woman whose life has centered
around what she does well knows that the reverse of that
equation holds the threat of exposure for what she does *not*
do well. If she feels most alive and worthwhile when she is
singing in a pink taffeta gown, then is she worth less if it
takes her a whole day to organize one walk-in closet?

This was Kay's predicament. Her mother-in-law knew
her in her housecoat—not in a taffeta gown. Someone
whose opinion she valued would catch her in the place of
her inadequacy. Then, in her mother-in-law's eyes, Kay
would see herself—not as a person who simply needed
some help and instruction in homemaking—but as a
woman who at the core of her being was deficient. She
would be seen as "less" of a woman. This is the experience
of shame.

Shame is a difficult topic to write or talk about. The
word *shame* is rarely even spoken above whisper level in
polite company. Shame is about hiding. It is especially
about hiding those parts of ourselves that hold the potential to elicit ridicule or criticism from others. In their eyes,
we will be seen—or known—as we really are and then
discarded. That is the fear in shame. As Dan Allender
has written, "All our elaborate defenses, disguises, and
personality traits are held in bondage to the goal of not
being known, because to be known is to be caught naked
and defenseless."[7]

The experience of shame, which is often below the

level of our conscious awareness, is much more than being embarrassed. Shame is closely akin to the word *mortified*, which comes from a French word meaning "death." Mortified means that on the inside, you want to curl up and die.

From our early experiences we learn that if we do this or say that we will feel deeply ashamed and that feeling is associated with a kind of death. Instinctively, we learn to avoid even the remotest possibility of further shame—like touching a hot stove only once, yet that is enough not to make the mistake twice. The sense of "death" that accompanies shame can also be experienced in a larger way. We let certain parts of ourselves "die"—our sexuality or anger or will or personal opinions, for example—rather than further risk the possibility of exposure to someone's hurtful gaze.

It is the downside of the grandiosity cycle—the fear of encountering shame—that provides much of the energy and momentum behind the tendency to overdo. Like a hamster on a treadmill, we keep pushing forward, exerting whatever effort it takes to feel as though we are staying ahead of where we were. Failure and criticism hold the potential for rejection—for feeling ashamed—and if we have to work doubletime to shore ourselves against that possibility, then we will march in place twice as fast as the next person.

"I was convinced that without the continual effort to excel," says Colette Dowling, "I had no hope of feeling even adequate. Flat out and unimproved, I was inferior stuff."[8]

As long as you can continue to live in the strong places where you feel acceptable, then the prospect of experiencing shame is so remote you may be unaware of its presence. Kay's life, for example, went smoothly as long as she could sing regularly. Good performances here and there were like buoys that kept her from sinking very far into a pool of shame and fear about her inadequacy as a homemaker and a woman. Her mother-in-law presented a crisis of exposure that pulled her down, literally, into the emotions she most wanted to avoid.

Sometimes you can go for years, for large portions of your life, unaware of the melancholic music that keeps you dancing as fast as you can. Often, you don't know what drives you so hard until some obstacle gets in your way. That obstacle or crisis takes many forms: someone no longer needs your help, your body refuses to keep up the pace, your success no longer satisfies. The ruse is up, and it's time to face the music.

It is interesting to note that the word *obsession* comes from a Latin root meaning "besieged." It speaks of the presence of fear or guilt. And fear, especially, is what breeds the excesses of compulsive living where we are not free simply to offer an honest effort as "good enough" or a helpful word that is merely helpful, not insistent. The one who is "besieged" is running away from an encounter with her own fear of inadequacy. She is hiding behind her "doing."

This is a significant part of why the lives of women who are devoted to helping, giving, achieving, and excelling take on a pseudo-masculine quality about them. The softer, more receptive parts of the way God made them are buried under "do-lists" that must get done and tasks that ought to be accomplished.

THE IMPOSTER PHENOMENON

When a significant portion of our success or overdoing is fueled by our hidden fears of being exposed as "less than," a diabolical inner conviction takes root. It has been referred to as the "imposter phenomenon."[9]

This label describes a secret belief (more common to over-achievers than under-achievers) that, in spite of their talents and abilities, they are *impostors*. Someday, a failure or slip-up will expose them for what they really are: a fraud. They can explain away their achievements or abilities with a variety of excuses: they got lucky, got by, or simply worked hard. Their real talent, if you will, lies in their ability to "fool" everyone into thinking they actually have some.

In one sense, the feeling of being an imposter stems from an inverted form of reasoning whereby your abilities seem commonplace simply because they are yours. The real talent appears to lie in what you can't do, rather than what you can. Occasionally someone will ask me what it's like to write a book in the same tone of voice used to address mountain climbers. I know how they feel. I look at the travel agent, who sorts through a myriad of details to get people on the right plane at the right time, with a sense of awe. I admire her ability because she is doing something I know I couldn't. But writing is different. Writing comes relatively easily for me. For that very reason, it is hard for me to consider it "talent."

But in another, deeper way, the feeling of being fraudulent is directly connected to the tendency to use our abilities as a cover-up for the shameful inadequacy we feel underneath. Our abilities and achievements harden into a mask that is used to keep others from discovering our hidden blemishes. Consequently, success, in its many forms, provides only surface pleasure. It never "sinks in" because it never really touches the real person underneath.

The inner sense of fraudulence only grows, as though we are carrying around a deep, dark secret that no one else knows. That's why the more we do, the more we have to do in order to keep from being "discovered."

SUMMING UP

This, then, is the invisible cycle that feeds the drive of women who are chronically prone to give out more than we take in. One part of us is saying, "You must be more, do more, have more," because there is another voice in the background chiding, "Unless you do, you will always be less." And so we push ahead when we need to pull back. We give until it hurts. We give out of our own emptiness—rather than the overflow of a full heart.

In the treadmill effect of overdoing, much of our creative, regenerative energy as women is lost to ourselves and to others. This is part of the tragedy of compulsive living. In overdoing, we become strangers to some of our innate attributes as women—our ability to receive from God and others, to enjoy, to wait, to relax in the shade of a strength that is not our own.

While our lives may be filled with activity and people, we are shriveled on the inside. And we have offered others caricatures of ourselves—thin, penciled stick figures who on cue move in and out of others' lives—rather than the whole, vibrant women, full of color and life, we were created to be.

Jesus called us to this kind of life—to the experience of finding our life in Him so we could give it to others with abandon. It is a giving and a labor that is not based on escaping anything—our fears or pain or insecurity. It is life and love as it has been given to us—freely, with no strings attached. His words in Matthew's gospel are hard to receive, yet meant especially for women like us:

> "Come to me, all you who are weary and burdened, and I will give you rest. Take my yoke upon you and learn from me, for I am gentle and humble in heart, and you will find rest for your souls. For my yoke is easy and my burden is light." (Matthew 11:28-30)

In a book such as this, it would be tempting at this point to begin to offer quick solutions to the problem of compulsive living. It would be easy to simply talk about a way to make life work better. "Here's a way to *do* your life differently." But such an approach would only wallpaper over the problems underneath. It would not effect real and lasting change.

It's strange that even when we deeply desire change, we also resist it just as strongly. Even when I knew the way I was living was no longer "working," for instance, I was tempted to just skate on and glide over the surface of the problem. I wanted to tidy up the edges of my life a bit and hope that would do it. But some small voice tugged at me: *Don't, Paula. Don't treat this lightly. Take a closer look at the anger, the resignation, the floating disappointment you carry around with you.*

Those were precisely the kind of emotional realities that I did not want to face. Part of my approach in life had been to avoid the confusing and the uncontrollable, and the world of feelings had the potential for both. Pondering anything very long seemed a waste of time. My instinctive reaction to troubling feelings had always been like that of Scarlett O'Hara: "I'll think about that tomorrow."

There are points in life, though, when for each of us the time is ripe. Tomorrow is now. And if we resist the urge to carry on as always, and turn instead to consider what is really happening inside us, change and growth happen in ways that are not forced.

That's why the next section of this book will explore some emotional roots of compulsive living. It will help us return to the places in our lives, in our original relationships, where we first formed our notions about what it meant to be a woman in a culture such as ours. As women, our most significant relationship in this regard is with our mothers. From her model and her mirroring of us, we learned our most enduring lessons about a woman's way of being in the world.

NOTES

1. Colette Dowling, *Perfect Women* (New York: Simon & Schuster, 1988), page 94.
2. See Genesis 3:7 and Acts 26:14.
3. Ellen Sue Stern, *The Indispensable Woman* (Toronto: Bantam Books, 1988), page 64.
4. Dowling, page 74.
5. Dowling, page 74.
6. C. S. Lewis, *Perelandra* (New York: Macmillan, 1949), page 87.
7. Dan Allender, *The Wounded Heart* (Colorado Springs: NavPress, 1990), page 48.
8. Dowling, page 21.
9. Joan Harvey, *The Imposter Phenomenon* (New York: Pocket Books, 1981).

PART · TWO

The Emotional Roots of Doing Too Much

CHAPTER SIX

Mothers and Daughters: Shared Identities, Common Quests

For you created my inmost being;
you knit me together in my mother's womb.
I praise you because I am fearfully
and wonderfully made.
PSALM 139:13-14

One day when I was about thirty years old, I was standing in line at the bank, waiting for the teller to process my deposit. In one of those small moments that slip past with little fanfare or notice, something happened that brought a slight, imperceptible gasp from my mouth.

It was the woman's reflection in the bank window I saw. Standing with one hand on her hip and another propping up her chin as she rested an elbow on a cold marble ledge, this woman was studying her surroundings with an inquisitive, thoughtful gaze. A cascade of dark brown hair framed her face. For a slight second, I was sure that woman was my mother. I was looking at my mother. What made me gasp was that the woman in the reflection was myself. For one disconcerting moment, I wasn't sure who was who.

Have you ever found yourself in a situation such as this where the way you looked or the words you said were "just like Mom's"? It's an uncanny feeling. You may be full grown and leading a separate life—yet, all of a sudden, it's your mother's voice you hear, her face you see in your own.

Mothers and daughters—is there any more basic human connection than this one? We are bound to our mothers by nature and nurture in an inextricable bond of femaleness. This is why any discussion of what motivates us as women who do too much must begin here—even if it ends elsewhere. A sizable portion of the energy that propels us forward originates in the ways that we have related to our mother.

What is it about the mother-daughter relationship that has such power to chart our course in life? To begin with, no human being has known us any longer than our mother. She was our whole world before we knew what world we were in. When we entered this one, it was her arms that first welcomed us. It's amazing how early, as little girls, we come to realize that we have a baby doll and *we are* our mother's baby doll. With her, we shared the world of pink dresses and hair bows. Unlike Daddy, we have bodies that can house people. We are women.

The importance of the mother-daughter relationship really hit home for me once I had a daughter myself. Until then, I had been skeptical of the idea that much of the way I went about life was a carryover from the way I related to my mother. That was ancient history, I felt. When I gave birth to a little girl, though, I began to see how much history repeats itself.

In Allison's face, I saw my own longings reflected without inhibition. I began to notice the way she watched my moods and expressions, how sensitive she was to my expectations. I saw how hard she worked to please me. I saw how even when she got mad and refused to do something I wanted her to, she was mad *at me.* Even her creating distance between us was a function of how close we were, as mother and daughter. A raised eyebrow, a sharp word—even small missteps on my part could easily wound her. Allison was mirroring back to me how much I had looked to my own mother (and my mother had looked to her mother) for affirmation and praise. For a warm embrace, a welcome smile from this significant woman.

Victoria Secunda wrote in her book about mothers and daughters,

> We depend on our mothers to conjugate our history, validate our femaleness, and guide our way. . . . [A] mother sets the tone for her daughter's life, provides a road map and role model, continues through the daughter's middle and old age to be her example.[1]

Our mother's model and her response to our emerging femininity play a major role in how we feel about ourselves as women. So, we naturally look to our mother to validate our passport to womanhood. That is part of the legacy of the mother-daughter relationship. The model of femaleness and the messages held therein leapfrog from one generation to the next, from mother to daughter in endless succession.

Let's examine four ways that some of our present excess energy and drive has its roots in earlier ways we related to our mothers.

OBSERVING MOTHER'S MODEL

If the truth were known, Cindy was secretly quite proud of her mother in many ways. Not many girls in her high school class had moms whose jobs could compare to being a branch manager in a state-wide banking institution. On the days when her mom picked her up from school, Cindy always hoped she would come inside to find her. Her mom looked sharp in a suit.

Cindy also wished that her mother could slow down some. It seemed like she lived in a state of perpetual motion—with work, meetings, carpools, and errands to run. Sometimes Cindy felt like she was intruding if she brought up seemingly trivial things. Goodness knows, Cindy had long ago learned to keep her emotional life to herself. When she was smaller and freer with her tears or anger, her mom would wring her hands. "Oh, that Cindy, she's so emotional, I don't know what to do with that child," she would say. As Cindy got older, she found it safer to write in her journal. Lately, she had joined a drama class at school. That was an outlet for her emotional life.

Cindy wondered, sometimes, what kept her mom going at her job. Cindy wasn't sure if her mom liked the work she was doing, or if she just kept pressing ahead to compensate for her husband's apparent lack of ambition. Cindy's dad had yet to make tenure in his teaching position. And while that was a minor setback to him, it had become a source of major embarrassment to Cindy's mother—and the subject of many arguments between them.

❦

What does a daughter learn from her mother about life? More than either of them would ever guess, it turns out. A daughter serves something like a twenty-year apprenticeship under her mother's model. And due in part to that famous female intuitive perception, not very much passes a daughter by.

In countless ways, daughters take their cues from mom. How does a woman feel about each of her children, about her home and her work, about the men in her life? Chances are her daughter *knows*, even if she lacks the ability to put her observations into words. Just as Cindy knew that her mother saw her father as weak and inadequate, most girls internalize their mother's perceptions of men and what they can hope to expect from the opposite sex.

"My mother was married to a successful professional man who was married to his job. I watched her become angrier and angrier as she tried—and failed—to engage this man," explains one daughter now in her forties. "I grew up feeling that no matter how hard you tried, men remained distant, forever outside a woman's orbit. You couldn't count on one for any real emotional support."

A daughter also carries a special barometer inside her that measures her mother's moods. To this day, when I hear my mother speak one sentence over the phone, I can give an almost instantaneous reading on how good or bad she's feeling. Most daughters, including my own, could say the same. It comes from years and years of watching your mother's face, listening to the exact tone in her voice so that you can gauge the mood she is in—and adjust yourself accordingly. As you study her, you tend to become more like her.

A mother's voice forms a maternal litany in a daughter's mind. You are shaped by her opinions, her advice, and her "hot-buttons," just as Cindy learned at an early age that her feelings made her mother nervous and irritable. She learned to hide that part of herself as unacceptable. A daughter hears her mother's voice—until finally, that voice is dubbed over her own, and the two become almost indistinguishable.

"No self-respecting woman would . . ."
"If you're going to do this right,

you need to do it this way . . ."
"Real women don't . . ."

If a mother is a positive role model, then she will be able to provide the proverbial "roots and wings" her daughter needs to feel adequate as a woman. Those emotional roots come from feeling nurtured by a mother who enjoys her. For all of a mother's efforts to civilize her daughter affirm her growth. A secure mother can take her daughter under her tutelage, allow her to fail, dust off her budding wings, and then help her gain the confidence that she, too, can soar on her own. A secure mother whose own life is spiritually grounded will do even more: She will serve as a strong bridge between her daughter and the Lord.

But if a mother is crippled by her own insecurities, then there is a female vacuum created in a daughter's life. The maternal voice in a daughter's mind lacks the warm, encouraging tone of a *mother*. Instead, that voice is something closer to a drill sergeant or a schoolmaster. The authentically feminine, truly nurturing model a woman needs instead takes *a false masculine form.* This false masculine voice is not the voice of a true mother, but a harsh, nagging critic full of "shoulds" and "oughts" and "musts."

This inner critic—the "unmother," if you will—is one significant part of what drives a woman so mercilessly, of what demands that she try ever harder to be perfect. This "masculine" voice is the one that pushes her so hard. "Try harder, look prettier, do more."

If, for whatever reasons, our mother was unable to "mother" us, then until we are able to receive God's grace in what we lacked, we may feel we have a shriveled capacity in situations that call for a feminine response. Being able to receive from others, to nurture, to lean on someone besides ourselves feels odd at best, and unbearably uncomfortable at worst. It shows up in many small ways. A child begs to snuggle on our lap, but we would prefer to sit alone. Our husband is sure that he can handle the laundry; we insist on doing it ourselves—so it will be done right.

For good or ill, in countless ways, our mother's model affects the way we approach life.

TRYING TO GAIN MOTHER'S VALIDATION

A second way we feel the impact of our mother is through her mirroring influence on our lives. We channel a portion of our energy and drive toward her recognition of us. Let me illustrate, for a moment, one way this happens.

When our children were small, a friend shared with my husband and me a helpful bit of parenting advice. "When you really want your children's attention," he told us, "get down on their level, take their face in your hands, look right into their eyes, and then speak. They will listen to you in a whole new way."

So when our daughter, Allison, was barely old enough to totter around by herself, I would cup my hands around her chubby little cheeks to tell her something I really wanted her to hear. "Allison, bring me your shoes." "Allison, it really is time to go to sleep now."

Sometimes, almost without thinking, I would find myself saying, "Allison, you are such a good girl. Did you know that?"

I really did not understand the power of my words until one day, Allison toddled over to my knee with her own hands cupped around her cheeks. She beckoned me to stoop down and hear what she wanted.

"Tell me I'm a good girl again, Mommy," she said, with big, expectant eyes. "Tell me I'm a good girl."

I looked at her and smiled. That was an easy enough request. "You are such a good girl, Allison," I replied. And with those words, her face broke out in a big grin, and she danced away again.

What Allison was doing that day—what all daughters do to some extent with their mothers—was to look into my face to try to get an accurate picture of herself. In a small, but very real sense, Allison knew who she was by what she saw mirrored in my eyes. Her words were the plaintive cry of every little girl to the woman in her life to whom she is bound by birth and rearing, by nature and nurture. "Tell me I'm a good girl, Mommy." *I want to be a good girl, Mommy. Somehow I can really believe I am, if I can hear it from your lips and see it in your face.* Allison was seeking my validation of her.

This is every girl's natural wish: to be seen and recognized as "good enough" just simply for who she is. As we grow up, it is to our mother that we most naturally look for such "mirroring." We long to be known by her, to be recognized and validated—not for something we have done or might do, not for the way we reflect on her—but for ourselves. A portion of our internal energy throughout our lives is expended in this direction.

This longing to be "seen" or recognized is one that little girls quite naturally exhibit. I remember sitting with a friend one Christmas as we watched a half-hour video of all her old home movies spliced together. In scene after scene, no matter what else was going on, there was Anne . . . dancing. Dancing on the front porch, dancing in the yard—always dancing. Before long, the two of us were doubled over laughing, just waiting to see if the next scene held any more of "dancing Anne." Only later did I realize that I had watched a visual metaphor for the longing of every little girl. In a deeper way, her antics were saying, "I'm here, can't you see? Can anybody *see* me?"

The longing to be seen, to be mirrored, is one that begins in relation to our mothers, but follows us throughout life. It's apparent in the way women seek out small clothing boutiques where a saleswoman has the time to assure them, "That dress looks great on you. That dress *is* you." Or I think even of the story of Mary and Elizabeth in Matthew's gospel: When Mary became pregnant with Jesus, she turned to Elizabeth to share the experience. With her, Mary would have another woman who could understand this womanish thing of carrying life inside her. In a variety of ways, women look to other women to validate them—just as they once looked to their mother to see themselves in her reflection.

In her mother's eyes, a daughter develops her first—and sometimes most lasting—impressions about who she is. With that innate wish to be *seen* by her mother comes a special grief when she is not. "My mother could handle only the parts of my life that were important to her—my achievements, my helpfulness, things like that. I learned to offer her just the parts of myself that I knew she wanted. Consequently, I never felt like my mother knew the real me," confides one daughter. Women have a deep need to feel that their mother sees their needs and weaknesses as well as their strengths—and that she can handle both.

The message we saw in our mother's eyes tends to follow us long into our adult lives. For some women, their mother's opinion of them forms a kind of secret truth that overshadows all others. "I made good grades and won a lot of awards," explains one woman, "but in my mother's eyes I could never measure up. I always had a real schizo feeling because the way I was seen 'out there' was not the way I was seen at home. I was never sure which was right." No matter what others thought of her, no matter how many awards she stacked up, she feared her mother's opinion of her would prove to be the correct one.

Early mirroring messages can be hard to overcome. Another woman told me that her favorite aunt, a strong mother-figure, pulled her aside one day when she was ten. Her aunt told her that it was too bad she wasn't a boy because she had such a good mind and a lot of ambition. Her aunt was apparently trying to find a gentle way to tell her that she'd better make the most of her brain because it was all she had! My friend says that to this day when someone tells her she looks pretty, she is sure they are making it up. It is hard for her to ever think of herself as "feminine."

The mirroring messages we heard growing up continue to play internal tapes inside our big girl minds. "You'll never be . . ." "I don't know why you ever thought you could . . ." "If I had your talent at the piano, I would have . . ." On and on they play, and somewhere inside us the little girl cries in a hundred different ways, "Tell me I'm a good girl, Mommy. Somebody please tell me." And so we perform and serve, we do and overdo, hoping that someday we will finally feel we measure up.

The deep longing to be "seen" and known as we really are is a legitimate need, one that is integrally a part of the way God made us. Ironically, when that unmet need is repressed and unrecognized, it dominates our lives in the driven need to prove ourselves.

The first time that I became emotionally aware of my longing to be "seen" occurred in the summer of depression that I wrote about earlier. Along with the depression I began to have dreams that storyboarded my life. One, in particular, I will never forget. I dreamed that I was caught in the stairwell of a building that was burning down around me. With tremendous effort, I crawled to safety. When I emerged from the ruins of this building, I was elated, like someone who had survived a holocaust. I went to present myself to the head foreman, to tell him I had made it out alive. But in the dream, before I could get the words out of my mouth, he took one look at me and said, "Oh, there's another dead one." And he stacked me in a pile of bodies to be buried.

I longed to run after him and get his attention. "I'm alive! I'm alive! Can't you *see* me?" I wanted to say.

It was an awful dream. But it gave me an emotional handle for my own longing to be seen and validated by someone else – to be *alive*. And when I could embrace the legitimacy of that longing, I could then hear, with special meaning, the words that David spoke of the Lord in the familiar Psalm 139:

> For you created my inmost being;
>> you knit me together in my mother's womb. . . .
> My frame was not hidden from you. . .
>> *your eyes saw* my unformed body.
> All the days ordained for me
>> were written in your book
>> before one of them came to be.
>>> (verses 13,15-16; emphasis added)

I had indeed been known – *seen* – by Someone who deeply loved me.

AVOIDING MOTHER'S EXAMPLE

When Gretchen thinks of her mother, the word *fragile* often comes to mind.

Her mother was a highly artistic woman, accomplished at the piano, skilled in writing, but her insecurities forever held her back in life, it seemed. She was temperamental and high-strung, given to bouts of depression that threatened to engulf the rest of the family.

Gretchen learned early how important it was to steer clear of anything that had the potential to tap into one of her mother's fears. In many ways,

growing up in her home was like walking through a
china store on tiptoe. When the mother was facing a
critical social function or piano recital, her husband
and daughters spent the weeks before trying to bolster
her confidence and get her ready. If she performed
poorly, then everyone had to pick up the pieces.

As Gretchen grew older, she became more
determined about one thing. "I will never be like my
mother," she quietly vowed. "I will never be incapacitated in life. I won't let my fears control me."

❦

For many women, the extra effort we expend comes not
from trying to measure up to our mother's expectations,
but from another source altogether. We may work doubletime to keep from duplicating our mother's life. We want—
desperately—to *avoid* her example.

In some ways, this pattern is just an inversion of
the theme of how much a daughter take her cues from
her mom. After years of watching her example, a daughter forms unconscious perceptions that shape her own
choices. Is Mom basically confident in her ability to handle
life? Is she secure enough to let herself lean on someone
else for a change—her husband, her friends, the Lord?
Does she avoid using her emotions to control everyone
around her? Is she happy? When the answer to questions like these comes back a consistent "no," and when
a daughter feels the weight of her mother's frustrated life,
she gravitates toward her polar opposite.

In Gretchen's case, when she rejected her mother's
example, she jettisoned the world of feelings and emotions
as well. It was a classic catch-22. In reacting to her mother,
Gretchen also let go of something vital in the way God

made her. She explained, "It was as if I determined that, since feelings could cause such problems and become so embarrassing, I just wouldn't have any. I came to feel like I had been neutered. I was not a woman—just a person out there accomplishing something."

Gretchen became a highly successful radio producer, doing far beyond what anyone demanded of her on the job. Her motto was "success at any expense." Moving ahead in her work was Gretchen's way of ensuring that she would not suffer from the same insecurities and unrealized potential that her mother had. She worked hard to keep her fears and inadequacies buried—lest her own emotional life rise to the surface and threaten to "take over," as her mother's had.

The irony was that the harder she worked, the deeper she stuffed her emotions, the more out of control her life became. When she gave birth to a daughter she began to face that the core of her workaholism had to do with her own mistaken efforts to avoid reliving her mother's life.

The woman whose excess drive and energy come from a subconscious attempt to avoid her mother's example is living a life of *reaction.* Though she may appear independent, in reality, she's tied to her mother. Her determination to be "different" may prevent her from being like her mother in obvious ways—yet, somehow, she never becomes herself either. She's stuck in a no-man's-land somewhere in between.

❦

PLEASING MAMA

When Ellen was a little girl she used to tell her friends that her father ran a car business. "But my mother, she runs us," Ellen would say, meaning herself and her two older sisters.

In a broad sense, Ellen was right. Her mom did a bit of volunteer work and some back yard gardening, but basically, she channeled most of her time and attention into her three daughters. She taught each of them to read while they were in kindergarten. By the time they each turned ten, she made sure they had one arena in which they excelled. One was a gymnast, the other could play the flute. And Ellen . . . she was known as "the pretty one."

Growing up during the Depression, Ellen's mom never had the opportunity to go to college. Nice things were a luxury in her family. So when spring came and she could dress each of her daughters in a new Easter bonnet, she was as thrilled as a child at the state fair. Her daughters' blue ribbons and trophies were displayed prominently on a special shelf in their rooms. Their good SAT scores were celebrated with a party. "Of course, you will go to college," she always said. Such things were just understood as a matter of fact.

It was not until Ellen was almost ready to enter graduate school that she began to question where this yellow brick road was taking her. She felt the need to find a park bench, so to speak, and rest awhile so that maybe she could get her bearings in life. Ellen loved her mother immensely. But while her mom had given her unflagging support and wisdom all these years, Ellen was beginning to see there was more to the picture. Her mother had been a great source of pressure as well.

❦

"If mama ain't happy, ain't nobody happy." That's an old saying you occasionally find framed on kitchen walls. It's a quiet reminder of how the emotional life of a home tends to revolve around the woman in the family. It is also an apt description of the way many of us feel: as though we have devoted large chunks of our lives to the task of "pleasing Mama."

There are two parts to this drama, this intricate waltz that mothers and daughters dance throughout their lives. One part belongs to the daughter. She looks to her mother for warmth and affirmation and a clear voice that says, "Yes, God has placed in your woman's soul something of infinite worth and value, and as your mother I want to be the first to give witness to that."

And Mother, what about her? We must not forget that Mother, the other partner in this feminine waltz, is herself a *daughter*. Every mother is someone's daughter. And as such, she had and still has her own longings and unmet needs, the inevitable wounds that come from living with imperfect people in a sinful world. The simple truth is that *the deeper the hole in a mother's heart, the greater her human tendency to look to her daughter, her children, to fill the empty spaces in her own life.*

A mother sees in her daughter the chance to set her own record straight. In her daughter's achievements, a mother's insecurities and missed opportunities can be repaired—or so it seems. In her lovely face, old wounds may be healed. "I was the jewel in my mother's crown," was how one woman phrased it. "She sent me, as her proxy, into the world to do the business that she hadn't been able to accomplish."

There is an enormous natural tendency for a mother to want to script her daughter into what *she needs* her to be, so that she reflects well on her.

When my daughter, Allison, was about four years old, in that stage where little girls can sit still for about ten minutes in a frilly dress, I remember taking her to visit one of the older women in the small town in Virginia where I grew up.

Before we went to visit Mrs. Randolph, I pulled Allison aside and coached her: "Mrs. Randolph's house is not the place to be a wild hyena. There are antiques in there and little glass pieces that can't be replaced. I want you to sit like a big girl and say 'Yes, ma'am' and 'No, ma'am.' Don't ask for a cookie. Don't play with the dog. Just sit and let us visit, and we'll go for an ice cream cone later."

Allison played her part well. Mrs. Randolph and I were able to visit in peace, and the dog went by mostly unpetted. Only as I reflect on that scene now, years later, does it strike me the extent to which I was depending on Allison, in that instance, to make up for a deficiency I felt in my life. When I was in high school, Mrs. Randolph would catch sight of me as I walked by her store and wave me inside with a smile. "Do you realize you are walking down Main Street with a big wad of gum in your mouth, Paula Sue?" she would say. Upon which I would promptly rid myself of that old pink wad in her wastebasket and hope against hope that someday, if I really worked at it, I might yet grow up to be a lady.

Allison's debut in Mrs. Randolph's living room was my quiet effort to say I had succeeded. Or more accurately, I had at least succeeded *with my daughter.*

This is some of the pressure we feel as we grow up and one part of the reason why we continue to perform and achieve and prove ourselves adequate. We are helping to set Mother's score straight, to gain her smiling nod of approval.

In a daughter's effort to please Mama—or even in her rebellion and determination to displease her—she often develops an "as-if" personality.[2] She becomes not her-self—the particular woman God made her to be—but some apparition of that. She allows herself to be molded and shaped by her mother's example and expectations—and in the process gives up the peculiar ground on which God has given her to stand. As Colette Dowling explained, "We settle for mother's involvement in our looks, our trumpet concerti, our skill at making puff pastry. We become what she needs us to become, developing those aspects of ourselves that she wants developed."[3] We do these things because it seems like the best route from our child's heart to hers.

These are some of the invisible chains that we wear around our feminine souls. These are some of the childhood strongholds that keep our patterns of overdoing locked in place. The route to freedom covers the painful ground of recognizing those emotional places where we longed for something we never quite received—especially from our mother.

When we can see our mother as a human being full of flaws and insecurities and half-met needs, we can begin to take our hand out of hers and put it in the Lord's.

The freedom that God offers comes as we are able to embrace our mother as a sister much like ourselves—a woman who doesn't want to grow old alone, a woman very much in search of One on whose strength she can rest her weary soul.

NOTES

1. Victoria Secunda, *When You and Your Mother Can't Be Friends* (New York: Delacorte Press, 1990), page 6.
2. Alice Miller, *Prisoners of Childhood* (New York: Bantam Books, 1987), page 12.
3. Colette Dowling, *Perfect Women* (New York: Simon & Schuster, 1988), page 209.

CHAPTER SEVEN

A Nightingale in a Gilded Cage: The Hero and Her Dilemma

By the grace of God I am what I am,
and his grace to me was not without effect.
1 CORINTHIANS 15:10

We must look in another direction in order to discover the emotional roots of performance-oriented living. That direction concerns the role that many of us learned to play in our original family, a role known as the *hero*.

A hero is the child in the family who carries the weight of making everything turn out as it should. Whether that child is a boy or a girl, the role requires a false super-human strength. It's the image of a knight in shining armor who faithfully comes to the rescue. It's the picture of the all-American fullback who pushes past every obstacle with whatever herculean effort is necessary to make the goal. To fall into the role as the family hero is to agree to project an image that all is well, no matter how you feel.

Every family is a small microcosm, a private corporation, a miniature world all its own. Each has its own fluid dynamics. Perhaps an accurate analogy for the family would be a collection of individuals, often related by birth, who find themselves together in a small boat traveling through the rough, uncharted waters we call life.

No matter how stable the craft may appear, each person knows capsizing is a possibility. There is a life-and-death quality to keeping the boat on top of the water and the water out of the boat. The important thing is to keep the family ship afloat.

Inside that lifeboat, a tenuous set of emotional checks and balances is kept. If one person is out of sync, through some form of unpredictable, aberrant behavior, every other passenger is affected. The whole situation easily becomes shaky. Alcoholism, workaholism, neglect, or abuse—an endless list of problems holds the potential to rock the boat. When that happens often enough, the family becomes dysfunctional and the supply of love and support keeping it afloat dwindles.

The more unstable or fragile the family becomes, the greater the need for someone to make up for the deficiency. Enter the hero.

Usually, the hero is the first person to realize intuitively that something is wrong with the family. Heroes are often firstborn children. The observant, in-tune feminine nature makes women good candidates for playing this role. A perceptive little girl can easily pick up the clues that her other siblings may miss: their parents aren't getting along, Dad is drinking too much, Mother is deeply depressed. Something is wrong. A little girl's means of coping with what she senses is, in the case of the hero, trying hard to be very, very good. Good in school, good at helping, good in everything.

The illusion is that somehow, by her good behavior, achievements, and awards, she can steady the boat and set it on course. She works very hard to reestablish balance. But because each person can be responsible only for his or her own behavior, the effort rarely pays off.

Three important ways and reasons become the motivations for a "hero" to try to save the sinking ship when a dysfunctional parent or family system threatens everyone's equilibrium. *Somebody* has to take action—and quickly— no matter what it costs her.

COMPENSATING FOR FAMILY WEAKNESSES

Alice was the first college graduate in two generations of her family. Her brothers had all pursued a trade, much like their father, while Alice set her sights on a career in journalism. Her parents were understandably proud.

Not until Alice was older did she make the connection between the increasing importance placed on her achievements growing up—and her father's struggles with his job and slow descent into depression. As she moved from high school into college, she became "the great white hope" walking through the family's front door. A little cloud of pressure followed her from junior high forward—a weight she carried into adulthood.

What had rested on her shoulders, she realized, was the pressure to compensate for her family's misfortune, especially her father's debilitating depressions. Her parents had lived their dreams through her. She had been the hero.

When a parent is struggling, a child who comes home with a super report card or who excels on the local basketball team can serve to soothe some of life's harder blows. The hero's achievements project a good impression. No family can be all bad when a child performs so well. According to author Sharon Wegscheider, a hero "provides those moments of hope and pride that even the most desperate of families experience from time to time, furnishing a source of worth for the family when all other sources have run dry."[1]

What happens in the hero-child is that she instinctively realizes there is more at stake in her efforts than simply winning the spelling bee or being chosen for the National Honor Society. Her efforts serve to compensate for all that is going wrong at home. The gap between the way things ought to be and the way things are is one she unconsciously strives to fill by her hard work. *Whatever tension may exist, at least everyone's happy when I perform especially well.* That's the unspoken perception of the hero-child, the reason she keeps pushing toward perfection.

In her book *No Longer the Hero,* Nancy LeSourd wrote,

> It was a funny thing about making all "A"s in high
> school. As each succeeding A piled up on the other,
> the pressure to achieve increased. It was no longer
> enough that I was good, or even very good. I now
> needed to be excellent, perfect, superlative . . . for
> the Hero, the desire to achieve is founded on the
> need to assure yourself that you matter, that you
> and your family have worth.[2]

The fine irony is that when the hero's great performance doesn't eradicate the problem at home, she just doubles her efforts, hoping against hope that someday she may finally do something that will somehow guide this ship to a safe harbor.

INSULATING THE FAMILY FROM PAIN AND CONFLICT

In families where some form of abuse is present, stability and emotional support are painfully absent. Into this void the hero-child enters, using her negotiating skills or keen sense of humor or whatever she can muster to soften the impact of the abuser. In a sense, she tries to become the foam rubber padding around the family's rough edges.

A professional decorator now in her late forties recalls the way she tried to act as the buffer for her father's rage attacks. The oldest of six children, she knew best how some slight thing could mysteriously transform him from a quiet, reserved man into a furious child. One minute he would appear perfectly reasonable, then something would set him off. Suddenly, he would be shouting obscenities and threatening to throw a plate. While her mother retreated in disgust and the younger children cowered in fear, his oldest child would take him on verbally for the fight. Her tenacity rescued her younger siblings from his wrath many times.

As she grew older, though, whenever she encountered the possibility of interpersonal conflict she vacillated between two extremes. She was either right there in the middle of it, even when she didn't need to be. Or she was shutting her door in retreat, too tired and confused to know what her genuine responsibility was.

Heroes who are drawn to insulate a family from the fallout of its dysfunctions are particularly prone to form triangle relationships. They become the referee between warring parents, or the negotiator between one parent and a difficult sibling. In either case, the hero often learns to live outside herself, so in tune with others' feelings and desires that she loses track of her own.

Children who adopt this role in the family easily slip into a pattern of role-reversal, where in substantial ways they parent their parents. Heroes often grow up before they were meant to or look back on their childhood, years later, and realize they never had one. At an early age they somehow knew that their parent was leaning on them, rather than the other way around. And the message they internalized and carried forward into the rest of life was the deadly, ruggedly independent one of a lone ranger: "I'm all I have in this world. It all depends on me."

❦

TRYING TO REDEEM

Helen was raised on the side of a mountain where a couple of families lived and watched their children grow up together. Her memory was chock-full of long summer nights when they played kick-the-can until dark and caught jars full of lightning bugs. When she forced her mind to think back far enough, her memories remained warm and nostalgic.

She never quite understood what happened with her parents about the time she entered senior high. It was a slow, steady descent from there on. The tension between her parents escalated. Her mother began to complain privately to Helen about her dad's lethargy and lack of initiative. Helen found herself caught between the two of them, explaining one to the other, arbitrating their "discussions." But no matter what she did, she was powerless to patch it all up. Like the slow, painful demise of a terminally ill patient, her parents' marriage fell apart step by step, inch by inch.

Helen's inner response to her family's disintegration was an unconscious move in the opposite direction. She lost twenty unwanted pounds, read a dozen self-help books, and eventually became a Christian.

She grew perfectionistic in her school work and increasingly choosy about the guys she dated.

> Whatever option lay before her—a new relation-
> ship, a career decision, even the car she bought—it
> became intensely important to "do it right." Exactly
> right. She was seeking a personal insurance plan of
> sorts, without knowing it.
>   Helen wanted to be perfect enough to guaran-
> tee that her future would not duplicate her past.
> She had already watched one family go down the
> drain—that was enough.

❦

One fear is above all others for a hero-child who watches
her family's ship begin to sink: that by some macabre twist
of fate, she will grow up and repeat the same scenario
again in her own life.

This is the avenue by which the hero takes on such
a heavy weight. Her efforts are focused on two fronts:
what she can do to redeem her present family situation
and what she must do to avert disaster in her own life in
the future. Her energy is poured into a herculean effort to
ensure that the future works out differently than the past.
Human nature longs for positive resolution. The hero is
desperately in search of the golden path that will ensure
a happier end to her story.

In trying to redeem her family, the hero-child functions in a number of capacities as part-time referee, coach,
counselor, and confidante. She develops amazing versatil-
ity. Always, though, she must be out in front—the scout
who can see trouble coming from any direction. Her job is
to head off problems at the pass, before they escalate out of
control. Whatever the need is, she must "fix it"—whether
other family members want help or not.

Because a hero's goals for her family are, in one sense,

noble and right, it is hard for her to see the issue of control that resonates within them. *I must keep this family ship afloat, otherwise we're all going to drown and die.*

"If only I could make my brother better, then I would be okay too. This family had to be restored. It was very important to me and I didn't understand why at the time. It had to happen. And I had to make it happen. God and me together."[3] This is the way LeSourd described her I-have-to-redeem-this-situation feeling as she grew up. Toward that end she prayed every night, often adding, "And please God, don't let me grow up and have a marriage like my parents'." As the situation deteriorated, she felt confused and hurt that God didn't step in and deliver her family in the way she hoped He would.

The hero-child whose energy is focused on redeeming her family and ensuring a different future for herself discovers, eventually, that her own sense of identity is wrapped up in the role of being the messiah. To save others (and thus herself) from impending shipwreck becomes her reason for being.

HOW THE HERO ROLE BACKFIRES IN ADULTHOOD

The child who learns to perform well, to cover up her own insecurities by trying to keep everyone else together, meets a round of applause that begins early.

As she matures, she reaps the rewards for her helpful spirit, for the way she takes on an impossible challenge. She stands tough when others would have given up. She hangs in there, giving and giving and giving, asking for little in return. Her talents are, by any measure, commendable. Her ability to pour oil on troubled waters is well-established. And who can fault hard work?

But as a hero grows older, confusion and disappointment take their toll in her. She begins to wonder, on some level at least, why she's so lonely, why life feels like such a dull, monotonous drag up a big hill. And in most instances, she hasn't reached her childhood goal. Her efforts weren't enough to keep the family ship on course. Her own life is not problem-free in the present. All the applause and reward hasn't brought the ultimate seal of approval she yearned for.

Adult "heroes" are very much like that little old lady who stared out of the television a few years ago in a hamburger commercial and asked, "Where's the beef?"

Playing the hero may have been the only safe, reliable script to follow growing up, but as you mature emotionally and spiritually, if you don't learn to let go, those tactics boomerang. What had been a survival strategy as a child often becomes a liability as an adult. The hero role has a disturbing tendency to backfire—especially in your work environment and in your personal relationships.

At Work

Family studies reveal that the adult hero all too often will find her way into jobs and community tasks that fit her fears—rather than her real talents. She stays with whatever brought her a measure of predictable success in the past, even if she would be better suited for something different. With so much riding on her performance as a child she learned to stay in safe, sure places where the fear of failure was minimal. Now as an adult, those places have worn into a rut. Many of her stronger talents lie dormant, waiting to be discovered.

Adult heroes are, in many ways, every employer's dream. They tend to be responsible to a fault, dependable, and hardworking. But their inability to know when to stop means that they are prime candidates for stress and burnout.

An adult who remains stuck in a hero role can be a difficult companion to work with as well. Failure of any sort or criticism threatens her. Because a sterling performance is so important to her, she can be relentless in her drive to perfect anything in herself or others that falls short. Being able to relax and enjoy success is not often found in her repertoire. It's hard for her to get around to having "fun."

In Personal Relationships
The adult "hero" is drawn, as if by a magnet, to relationships with weak, dependent people who need her. Because her own needs are so shameful to her, she knows very little about receiving love and help from others. Often, without knowing it, she encourages irresponsibility and weakness in those closest to her.

Romantically, the woman stuck in this role tends to match up with men who need remodeling. She is drawn to the man who needs to be rescued, who—with her help— can finally become the godly, caring man he ought to be. This is the kind of man she connects with, if she connects at all.

Women who have grown up in fragile families that were falling apart often construct a fantasy man—their own knight in shining armor—who will invade their lives and become all their dads were not.

This unattainable ideal is the stuff of fairy tales. But then, that's what it would seem to take to right the wrongs of the past. They remain, for years, a damsel waiting for a knight. As Nancy LeSourd explains,

> This Cinderella was waiting for her prince to make up for her past. The man who could fit the glass slipper and win my heart became larger than life. The longer I waited for this man, the more amazing he got. This man would make up for all the hurt in the past. He would be a marriage partner who surpassed all others. He would love me for who I was and accept me. He would, in essence, be perfect at all times.[4]

In comparison, a normal relationship with a man is a disappointing letdown. Adult heroes often pass up, as a result, a number of relationships that hold wonderful potential for real intimacy.

Inside close relationships is the place where our unwillingness or inability to let go of our hero posture exacts its greatest toll. Close relationships require authenticity. They require, by definition, that others know us as we really are—in our weak moments, our times of confusion and need, in our sin. Times when we are *anything* but a hero. If we remain hidden behind our mask, we will never be able to utter the redemptive words that every relationship demands from time to time: "I'm sorry, I was wrong"; or "I'm frightened and confused. Please help me."

If we must always be seen in our best light, we will panic when criticism or unwanted exposure threatens to blow our cover. If we must always be the hero, we will never be known or deeply touched by someone else.

AWASH IN AMBIVALENCE

Perhaps the strongest feeling that a hero-child carries into adulthood is that of being special. To be a family's messiah-in-pigtails—the one who somehow manages to make things, if not right, then at least a little smoother—is a powerful role to play. She has an important place in the scheme of things. Many a hero-child will say as an adult reflecting on her childhood, "Well, there were problems at home, sure. And my parents had a lot of needs. But I always knew I was *loved*." What she means by "love" is closer to this: *The hero knew that she held a special place in the family because her efforts or achievements were desperately needed.* The feeling of being needed is as close as she could get to the feeling of being loved.

In adulthood, though, that feeling of being special is fraught with ambivalence. For underneath that specialness, a destructive paradox exists. And as we grow older, we intuitively recognize its presence even if we can't name the problem.

We are caught in a bind. On one hand, we feel special, tremendously needed, at times even grandiose about our capabilities. And we are rewarded in tangible and intangible ways for our performance. But on the other side of the coin, in our most honest moments, we feel worthless and, on a deep level, abandoned and ignored.

This ambivalence originates from our old family contract, one that we should never have been asked to sign: "In exchange for a place in this family, I am willing not to be myself. I will be the hero, if that's what you need for me to be. I'll do whatever it takes to belong."

The hero-child agrees not to be who she really is in any way that conflicts with the image of the good girl. Yet even good little girls sometimes cry and get angry. The best occasionally fail. Not even "perfect" ones can keep their act together all the time.

Real living includes a whole range of feelings and behaviors outside the narrow confines of being a "hero." Depending on how much freedom is present to explore those, the hero role, in its most extreme forms, is the moral equivalent of abandoning your own soul. The message the hero-child internalizes is that she must not be who she really is. Only those parts of herself that perform well—that keep the fragile peace—are valuable. In the deepest parts of her soul, she feels prostituted.

A subtle fear takes root: "If I was anything other than the 'hero' in this family, this ship would go down. Or even if it didn't, I would have no real reason to belong on board."

As an adult, the need to feel "special" produces a vicious cycle. You have to be special to feel worthwhile. Yet trying to be exceptional also places you in the position of being different and aloof. The loneliness, the isolation of such a perch, drives you to want deeply to feel you truly belong. But that prospect has problems, too. It's painful simply to join the human race as an ordinary, normal person. When we do that, we lose some of our sense of "specialness." And specialness is the only connection we have known to being worthwhile. We have become, as the title to this chapter suggests, a nightingale in a gilded cage.

A nightingale in a cage can sing beautifully, but her song seems to serve only to keep her separate and alone. This is how the adult hero comes to feel: as though she is special in a way, but this strange "specialness" keeps her trapped. She has been handed an award only to find out it was a booby prize. Being "special," being the hero, means that you don't ever get to be yourself. You don't ever get to have real needs like everyone else. You aren't allowed to be a normal person. The more you win . . . the more you seem to lose.

Sometimes, when the inner pressure has mounted for many years, a woman will unknowingly sabotage herself. Perhaps by her depression, or a career "failure," or anger that spins out of control—something will happen that addresses directly the question she has always avoided. Is there anyone in my life who sees me and knows me and yet loves me as I am, *for no good reason at all?* Will there ever be someone who recognizes that this nightingale is missing a few feathers and that a spot under her wing is hurting and sore?

When remaining stuck in the role of superwoman proves to be more painful than beneficial, when the liabilities start to outweigh the advantages, the adult hero finds herself in a merciful place.

It is possible—wonderfully possible—that the nightingale in her may yet discover she can fly. From her wounded, lonely perch she will see that the door to her gilded cage has been set ajar. The big wide world of real life and love waits to be explored.

❦

We have discussed two ways that our patterns of perfectionism and indispensability are set in motion through our early experiences. Unrealized longings for the deep affirmation of a parent, especially our mother, is one important influence. The hero-to-the-rescue effort you may have played in your original family is often another.

From these two sources a reservoir of pain collects. That pain, on a deep emotional level, is really one of feeling rejected for who you are or as you are. Such pain produces a deep wound of the spirit.

What happens in emotional wounding is very similar to what takes place on a physical level. If you burn your arm, for instance, you will do everything possible to avoid contact with the injured limb. Your instinctive response is to shield yourself from any more pain. You may hide the wound beneath a protective bandage. You may cover it with a salve. But in one way or another, you will tend to favor the wound to protect yourself from further injury.

In the emotional realm, our instinctive response is much the same. We are prone to cover our wounds, to shroud them in soothing secrecy until after a while we are no longer even aware of the pain beneath our compulsive behavior. We work doubletime to make sure that criticism or incompetence does not reopen old hurts and leave us unprotected and exposed. All the while, those wounds remain supercharged with sensitivity, cut off from the spiritual and relational resources that would enable them to heal properly.

Because the pain is buried deep, it is never addressed. What we know about God and many of the great truths in the Bible stay stuck in our heads—far removed from the broken, hurting places in our lives. They do not reach our hearts. As long as our energy is devoted to protecting ourselves from further pain—to favoring the wound—much of the liberating power of the gospel is lost to us.

In the next chapter, we will continue to explore what this kind of hiding costs us and those around us.

NOTES

1. Sharon Wegscheider, *Another Chance* (Palo Alto, CA: Science and Behavior Books, 1981), page 13.
2. Nancy LeSourd, *No Longer the Hero* (Nashville: Thomas Nelson, 1991), pages 63-65.
3. LeSourd, page 98.
4. LeSourd, page 141.

CHAPTER EIGHT

The Little Girl in the Cellar: Why We Hide

Surely you desire truth in the inner parts;
you teach me wisdom in the inmost place.
PSALM 51:6

Rachel was a well-respected teacher in a local high school. Parents of seniors competed to get their children into her twelfth-grade government class. She had a reputation for being able to teach kids how to think conceptually—and that, the parents knew, was no small feat.

It always surprised Rachel a bit that others thought of her as such an intelligent woman. Oh, she knew she was bright enough. She had excelled in school without that much effort. Her mind was her one reliable resource. It was her capital, so to speak, the linchpin of her personality on which she built the rest of her life. Even her relationship with God revolved around studying and systematizing the truths she learned.

There were occasional moments when Rachel saw the irony of being known as such a smart woman. As a little girl, she had been the neighborhood space cadet. "Oh, Rachel lives in another world, you know," her brothers used to say when she was late or she had lost something. Rachel could get so engrossed in the abstract world of ideas that she lost track of time and she never knew where she laid anything down. Her mother was an accountant, and her brothers grew up to be financial planners. As "bottom-line" people they had little understanding or patience for the kinds of ideas that fascinated Rachel.

In some ways, Rachel still saw herself through their eyes. She often felt like a foolish little girl who didn't have enough sense to keep her act together. She lived with the fear that one of her students' parents would someday discover her inadequacy with the detailed side of keeping track of grades and papers.

Part of her was intelligent and ambitious, while another part bordered on inept. She was capable in some situations, klutzy in others. She was afraid that one day, if she let down her guard, her klutzy part would come out of hiding and destroy a reputation she had spent years building.

❦

Keeping the klutzy part of herself hidden and out of view was a major factor in what drove Rachel so hard in her job. She couldn't risk the ridicule she felt was sure to come if others saw her as less than super-accomplished. Competence and knowledge were the hallmarks of her personality. Even her relationship with God was primarily cognitive, one dimensional.

In the previous chapter, we talked about the way we "favor our wounds." This reflexive effort to shield ourselves from further pain has two effects: (1) It leads to a fractured personality where we disown the "unacceptable" parts of ourselves; and (2) it fosters the creation of a "superself," an idealized fantasy image of the woman we wish we were.

BANISHING OURSELVES TO THE BASEMENT

When our personality is fractured, we lose access to vital aspects of who we are—our true feelings, needs, and vulnerabilities. We "lose ourselves," but not in the way that Jesus intended when He said we must first lose our life to find it. As C. S. Lewis explained, Christ meant something very different by the phrase "losing yourself." He meant that His disciples must abandon "the clamour of self-will; once they have done that, He really gives them back all their personality, and boasts . . . that *when they are wholly His they will be more themselves than ever before*"[1] (emphasis added).

Losing ourselves illegitimately begins in childhood when we learn which parts of ourselves are valued and praised—and which bring criticism, ridicule, or a blank stare. Most little girls, notes Harvard psychologist Carol Gilligan, are confident and self-assured until the age of eleven or twelve. But during our teens we begin the sometimes lifelong process of accommodating ourselves to the image of the "perfect girl," doing whatever it takes to be liked and accepted by others. In the process of becoming a chameleon, we lose our true colors.

Having a fractured personality is a lot like living in a house with a dark cellar beneath it. On the first floor, in the part of the house you keep presentable and decorated for company, your adult self resides and entertains. Here you give space to all the aspects of yourself that others have admired and wanted and found acceptable. You create a "self" out of some combination of your perceived strengths—your beauty or brains, your helpfulness or capacity for work, and a special talent. You bend and shape yourself into someone you think others will want.

But the cellar part of this house—of your personality—is kept well out of anyone's view. Cellars are dark, damp places where all the discarded stuff gets cast aside—things that seem too ugly, useless, or unwanted to be given a place in the rest of the house.

In the cellar of our fractured personality lives a little girl who embodies all the rejected, unacceptable parts of ourselves. This little girl does not shine at anything very special. She represents whatever aspects of ourselves, for one reason or another, we have orphaned—our sexuality, power to make choices, ability to feel deeply. These are all the places where we experienced pain or ridicule in the past. In Rachel's life, for example, she banished to the cellar the very human aspects of being dependent on someone else for the expertise that she lacked. Whenever it seemed she might be caught needing something from others, she felt foolish.

In Rachel's mind, those dependent aspects of herself seemed more foolish and ugly and repulsive as she chose to ignore their reality. *That's what happens to any aspect of ourselves that gets cast into the cellar.*

All of Rachel's energy was devoted to sprucing up the first floor of her house, so to speak, where she was determined to stay. That was why she relied so heavily on her mental abilities: They were her hedge against having to face that dependent, needy self who lived in cramped quarters in the cellar.

Those of us for whom some form of "doing" is the hallmark of our lives will find that we relegate different parts of ourselves to the "cellar." The part of myself I tended to deny was my feelings. I remember a time when a good friend challenged the way I looked at the emotional side of life. "Why, in the five years I've known you, Paula, have I never seen you cry?" she asked. I shrugged my shoulders.

I had little use for tears, that was true.

"What good are feelings?" I responded truthfully. "It seems like they only slow you down."

I understood very little, at the time, of the role that feelings—joy, anger, sadness, any of them—were meant to play in the whole of life. If the self in my cellar ever shed a tear, I didn't want anybody to know about it. That was part of the "fracture" in my personality.

WHOLENESS: AN INNER SYMPHONY

A fractured personality is quite contrary to the way God made us. It's not what He had in mind. We can see this in the Hebrew word for "soul" (*nephesh*), which means "the essence of a person in his or her wholeness." God sees our soul, our self, as an integrated whole.

God relates to us in much the same way a conductor looks at a symphony before him. That is a fair analogy, I think. He stands ready to incorporate the soft, lilting strain of violins, the passionate clang of cymbals, the bold, vibrant sounds of horns, the steady, resonant chords of the cello—whichever part adds the needed contribution to the whole, the right note at the right moment. In a similar sense, there are as many varied aspects to the way God made us as there are instruments in an orchestra. Parts of us are gentle and tender as a Brahms lullaby. Others are passionate, daring, and strong. God's intent is that our lives should resonate with a full chorus of the particular music He placed in our souls.

If we had grown up in the Garden of Eden—in an ideal environment where all our needs were perfectly met—we would have experienced all the legitimate aspects of the way God made us. To be made in His image is to be created with the capacity for a number of wonderful things: creativity, rationality, an ability to feel deeply, maleness or femaleness, a longing for intimacy, a desire for God, an appreciation for beauty. God created us to know life in Him as whole people where all the aspects of our being are deeply embraced and joyfully offered to others. As His creation, we bear God's indelible image imprinted on our souls with the capacity to become—not divine—but fully human.

We become more whole, more "fully human" by living in growing dependence on God. And while we will not experience the reality of the completed wholeness we were meant for until we get to Heaven, still this is the direction that God is moving us toward even now. It is part of the process of maturing spiritually. Both the Old and New Testaments declare that our goal is to learn to love God with all our heart and soul and mind, with our whole self.

In Luke 10:38 we can see this process taking place in the life of Martha, one of the most notorious of all overdoers. She was a woman many of us can deeply identify with: a decisive, get-things-done kind of person who orchestrated everything around her. I am moved by the fact that Jesus did not reprimand her for being in the kitchen doing what she did so well. He simply drew her attention to the contemplative, "being" side of life that she had ignored in all her busy efficiency. It is as though He said, "Come see the part you have missed all these years, dear Martha. Come sit here with Me awhile."

God's purpose is not that any legitimate human aspect of the way He made us be relegated to the cellar of our existence. His intent is to fling open the windows of our house, unlock the cellar door, and invite the little girl who represents all the abandoned, unwanted aspects of our souls to come upstairs and breathe fresh air.

STRIVING FOR OUR OWN VERSION OF THE IDEAL

The second effect of burying emotional pain, "favoring the wound," is that we tend to create a superself personality, an idealized fantasy version of the woman we wish we were.

In living splintered, fragmented lives, we pick out a few "acceptable" parts of our personality and build our life around them—sometimes to exaggerated proportions. Whatever that special ability is has a tendency to become the cornerstone of our identity. It's like listening to a theme song in a movie played over and over until the other music fades into the background.

When we live out of the few acceptable parts of our personality, we end up creating a facade that is not real. This facade is what some have called a false self, a "superself."[2]

&

Faye walked out of her bedroom, and the first thing she saw was last night's dishes, still in the sink. She fought the urge to go back to bed. But the girls were already up, watching cartoons, and she had a million things to do.

She felt a little more hopeful after she dressed. Today was the day Faye had set aside to get her house back together again. After a couple of weeks of meetings and appointments, one thing after another it seemed, she finally had a day to attack the clutter. Then the phone rang.

"Faye, I hate to call you this early," the voice on the other end began. "But we are desperate to get this month's newsletter in the mail, and Diane is sick and can't come in today. Do you think you could come, even for the morning?"

Faye thought for a moment. After all, she was on the board of this organization and she believed in their cause. To her knowledge, she had never turned

down a legitimate request for help. Faye liked that
feeling of knowing that others could count on her.
What good reason did she have for saying no? The
clutter could wait one more day, she guessed.
   Trouble was, it had been waiting for months. . . .

❦

Faye's life has been centered around her ready accessibil-
ity to other people's demands on her time. Her friends
think of her as superwoman. What they see is a woman
with a whole portfolio of abilities. She can raise money,
motivate a team of workers, work tirelessly on needed
projects. But what she never lets anyone see is the Faye
whose day-to-day life is as cluttered and overwhelmed as
her kitchen sink. She seldom allows herself the freedom to
stop and get her own life in order.

Whatever shape this superwoman fantasy takes in
our lives, it is always larger than life. A superself is an
idealized version of our real self with our strengths mag-
nified and our flaws finally fixed, or at least made presentable. Faye's version of this false ideal was that of being
a woman of inexhaustible resources. A woman who could
come to the rescue of whatever problem presented itself.
The illusion is that if we could just reach this false ideal,
then we would finally gain the love and acceptance that,
for one reason or another, have eluded us.

Few of us are conscious of the fantasy self we carry
around. At least I never was. I knew that my anger tended
to erupt at unpredictable moments and that disappointment dogged my trail no matter what I was doing. Why
couldn't I have done that article just a little better than
I had? Why did I recoil when my daughter wanted me
to stop my motion and empathize with her pain at not

being able to find a close friend in third grade? These kinds of hints littered my life like crucial messages written in Morse code. I could not read them because of the fear—the terror—that if I stopped, if I felt, if I settled for being good instead of great, I might not reach the goals that this fantasy woman painted on oversized murals in the back of my mind. I might remain all of my life as less than perfect.

The irony was that I had never considered myself a perfectionist. In my mind, no one who blotted her lipstick on check stubs or changed the sheets before company and major holidays rated such a label. But I slowly began to realize that in any arena defining my particular version of the ideal I longed to be—my version of superwoman—there I was indeed a perfectionist. I didn't dare slow down and face my very human reflection.

When we are living with the reality of a false ideal, a superself, our lives tend to be ruled by what David Seamands calls "the tyranny of the oughts."[3] *I ought to be able to live out the ideals of my fantasy self but I cannot. I should have . . . I could have . . . if only.* Hence anger and frustration, subdued rage, and eventually depression surface when the evidence of failure or weakness or inadequacy crosses our paths.

Over time, our false self hardens into a mask that turns into a prison. This is tragic on two counts. On a personal level, the masks of our superself imprison us in lonely isolation.[4] Whatever praise or admiration comes our way seems to be handed to this superself personality, not to us. It never touches us on a deep level. Yet in the process our real self—the person God declared eternally valuable—becomes more elusive. Though we may continue to excel on the outside, our inner life remains stuck in the same place.

The aspects of our true personhood that we have confined to the "cellar" remain there, undeveloped and immature. This is some of the pain behind that common statement, "I know I just turned forty. But I don't feel grown-up yet." For many of us, that's true. Significant aspects of what it means to be a fully functioning adult—a whole person—are still frozen beneath the surface of our hyper-lives.

Yet the bondage of an idealized false self profoundly affects our relationships as well—in ways that may take us years to fully realize. Our false ideals are, in reality, determined means of keeping others at arm's length. We are afraid of being seen as we really are. And the energy required to keep the structure of our false superself in place is tremendous. It's like a harsh taskmaster demanding we stay on guard, causing us to forever stand at attention, lest we get caught with the slip of our imperfections showing. *The energy that would be and should be channeled into loving others is siphoned off into creating an illusion of personal security.*

This is where sin enters the picture. There is a slippery slope between our own wounds *and hurting others.* Out of our own wounds come our worst offenses. Isaiah makes that plain in the way He prophesied about Jesus Christ's sacrifice:

> Surely he took up our infirmities
> and carried our sorrows. . . .
> But he was pierced for our transgressions,
> he was crushed for our iniquities;
> the punishment that brought us peace was
> upon him,
> and by his wounds we are healed. (53:4-5)

In His death, Jesus carried all our hurts—and He also bore the curse of our sin, the hurt we've inflicted on others.

How do others feel in our presence? That can be the ultimately revealing question for us. Do they sense an invisible barrier that can't be scaled, no matter how hard they try? Would they feel chronically "missed," as though when they bring up a difficult topic, suddenly we pull away in retreat?

Or worse yet, are there people in our lives who could honestly complain of being used? People who feel that as long as they make us look good or feel needed we want them around? That's where an attachment to a superself image—no matter how noble or good it appears—ultimately leads.

For in our own imprisonment, we invariably enslave others to our hidden agenda. As Nancy Groom explained, "From behind the bars of our self-protective pretense we cannot offer freedom and love to anyone else. . . . If we free them to be themselves, they might let us down. If we love them for who they are, they might not change into who we need them to be for our benefit."[5]

I flush pink with embarrassment and sadness to think of the friends and family members who have suffered from the fallout of my determination to be seen in the best light. Tragically, I know that I have hurt most deeply those I love most. I can sit through Sunday school week after week, for instance, but let my husband decide to teach, and suddenly he needs to glow in the dark.

I remember well a time when we returned home after a particularly difficult session where no one said much and one man yawned throughout. We had scarcely shut the front door before I began to give Stacy a list of suggestions for improvement. He looked at me for a moment, then he turned his head in a gesture of hurt and defeat. "It was only a class, Paula, not the World Series."

When he left the room, hot little tears trickled down my face. Tears of remorse that I had lived so long this way, choosing to burden someone I loved rather than release my grip on this false notion of perfection I held so tightly.

Such is the way we use others, offering them in the

sacrifice and service of our impossible ideals, our "super-self," rather than loving them for who they are. Using them in this way is the opposite of love. When we face that squarely we may have found our deepest motivation to change.

NOTES
1. C. S. Lewis, *The Screwtape Letters* (New York: Macmillan, 1949), page 59.
2. David Seamands, *Healing Grace* (Wheaton, IL: Victor Books, 1989), page 64.
3. Seamands, page 98.
4. Nancy Groom, *From Bondage to Bonding* (Colorado Springs: NavPress, 1991), page 97.
5. Groom, page 97.

Our Greatest Need: To Discover an Unreasonable Love

*How great is the love the Father
has lavished on us,
that we should be called children of God!
And that is what we are!*
1 JOHN 3:1

Our natural human tendency to hide behind our talents and to protect ourselves against anything that undermines our established sense of identity may seem safe and reasonable. But it costs us—and those around us—dearly.

Women for whom performance or pleasing others is paramount know the quiet terror of relinquishing the false props on which we have relied. But let go we must. Living behind a facade is not merely inconvenient or unhelpful, it is wrong, because it avoids any real encounter with God or other people in our lives.

FLUSHED OUT OF HIDING

Mary turned sideways before the mirror and groaned. *Where did that disgusting little tummy come from?* she wondered. Here she was almost forty-three, single with no children, and she had to take a deep

---

breath and squeeze in her stomach like the bottom of an accordion. She sighed with a heavy note of regret. Lately, the signs of an aging body stood out to her at every glance in the mirror. It was like becoming slowly invisible, she felt. The attractive, energetic woman she had always known herself to be was slipping slowly out of reach.

"Oh, just get on with it," Mary told herself half out loud. Hastily, she applied her lipstick and stuffed the last remaining loose items in her purse. A small mountain of work was waiting for her at the office. The sales meeting that she had given her new administrative assistant to organize was back on her own do-list, by Mary's choosing. When she had seen how inexperienced her assistant was in planning for a crowd of people, she decided she'd rather do the whole thing herself than coach someone.

"Give her a chance," her boss had said, but Mary didn't want to risk any slip-ups. "Oh, all right, then, if you insist," he'd given in. She remembered his smile. "You know why we jokingly call you, 'Mary, Mary, quite contrary,' don't you?"

What frustrated Mary was not just that she had the arrangements for this big weekend conference back on her desk. She was starting to realize that she simply couldn't keep up this pace much longer. Yet she was also afraid of backing off her superwoman status—more afraid with every wrinkle, every gray hair. What did she have left if she let up?

❦

Each of us has years invested in an image of ourselves that we cherish. Being competent or beautiful or supremely helpful—these are some of the ways that we've made it as far as we have in life.

But as we grow older, life itself seems to chip away at the superstructure around which we've built our identity. For the achieving, push-ahead woman this turn of events often comes, as it did for Mary, in the form of an obstacle in her path that she cannot overcome by more determined effort. Mary was staring in the face of physical limitations that would force her to live at a slower, more normal pace. The indispensable woman's turning point usually comes in a more subtle way. She may be the only one who notices the problem. Her involvement in everyone else's needs turns into a chronic sense of feeling overwhelmed with life and responsibility. She longs to join the world rather than carry it around on her shoulders like Atlas.

However this dismantling process happens, though, it usually takes us by surprise. It is especially hard for those of us who have relied on God to help us reach our phantom ideals of perfection. God no longer seems like an ally in the fight to reach a continually moving goal. Instead, it appears as though He is standing in the way as we are led deeper into the territory of our worst fears: helplessness, defeat, and inadequacy. God seems to become almost an enemy as He peels away the masks we have hidden behind.

God's way of dealing with the pain in our lives is to reveal the extent of our wounds so that He can carry us *through* the pain. He pierces the wound, so to speak. He drains it of its hypersensitivity and frees us from the compulsive need to hide and protect ourselves. We will always carry the scar, but it is no longer so raw and tender, infected with fear.

When God addresses the superstructure around which we've built our identity, He is tearing the pretense away. He calls us to come out of hiding; He exposes our prodigal paths. This is, essentially, a wonderfully hopeful process—even though it can be frightening at times. For in the midst of it, we are forced to address the unresolved, unvoiced questions left hanging in the back of our minds. *When I don't do well, when I have next to nothing to offer, when I am not smart or capable, will I be loved, then? Will I matter to anyone?*

During the period of my life when I sensed that it was impossible to hold on to my images of youth and super-competence, God seemed particularly absent. No matter how much "spiritual activity" I participated in, a confident faith (as I had known it) became more elusive. God seemed so much less predictable than before, and that unnerved me. I was having to relinquish "faith" as a set of propositions and embrace a relationship with Someone who was calling to me in much the same way God had addressed Adam in the garden. "Where are *you*, Paula?" It was like being flushed out of hiding. Or to use a good friend's descriptive phrase: "I felt like I was dancing with a Lion."

This kind of discomfort is meant to lead us somewhere. It takes us back to where we started, to that original first blush, just-as-I-am encounter with God. Through the back door, it seems, we will have fallen into a fresh sense of feeling loved by God.

WHO CHRIST DIED FOR

If you think back to your first experience of God's grace, perhaps you remember the same wonder at being forgiven that I felt. The gospel is, as George MacDonald claimed, news that is too good not to be true.

What amazes me, though, is how quickly I gave up that ground. Inch by inch, I retreated to more familiar territory. Before long, *what I did* became the paramount issue in life again, eclipsing the experiential reality of a love I could never earn. It's that way for many of us, I think. Before the ink on the baptismal certificate is dry, we're back at it again, straightening up ourselves, dusting off the shelves until our internal house seems in order, so we can invite God into the parlor where everything looks nice enough for company.

As the years rolled by, I enlisted God in much of my determined effort to be the perfect woman. I learned how to study the Bible and how to communicate with my husband, how to share my faith and raise children who sat still through church. Many of those "how-to's" turned into golden hoops that I jumped through, until finally I ran out of energy and motivation to go at it again. I remember turning to my husband one day and throwing out a question that seemed to slip out of my head sideways. "Why do you think God makes it *so hard* to serve Him?" I asked. I was worn out from the effort.

By this point in life, I had taken to retreating to a convent outside of town for a couple of days once or twice a year. I thought of those times as a "refilling" station— meaning, unfortunately, I gathered the courage to go back and try harder again.

One afternoon I turned to a passage in Matthew's gospel I had not read in years, the classic words of Jesus: "Come to me, all you who are weary and burdened, and I will give you rest. Take my yoke upon you" (11:28-29). In an uncharacteristically honest moment, I turned to the Lord and admitted the truth: "God, evidently I don't believe a word of this. You and I both know it. These words might as well be written in invisible ink."

Immediately a thought came to me. What had I believed? How had I been finishing that phrase? "Come to Me . . . *and I will give you a great big job to do.*" That's what I had really believed. God had become just one more person whose high expectations I tried to meet.

That insight was just one of many, many others over

a couple of years in which God exposed the illusions and false pretenses with which I'd approached life. The same front, the same superwoman that I presented to others was the one I offered God most of the time, asking Him to endorse my creation and baptize my big dreams.

I finally began to see that *He loved me enough to refuse to cooperate with my misguided goals.*

What I'd come up against was an immovable reality. God seemed utterly unpleasable. I'd done it as "right" as I knew how. I'd tried to be a good girl, and it wasn't enough. I felt absolutely empty-handed. I wanted to turn my face to Heaven and say, "What does it take to please You, Lord? Why can't You be pleased?"

And that was precisely the point, I found. He couldn't be pleased. I was in an emotional place where I could finally hear His message: *When you were nobody special, Paula, I loved you. When you had nothing to offer Me—not a thing—I received you. I called you My daughter when you felt foolish and insignificant. I made you Mine.*

The little girl inside me who felt failure and weakness, the one who had unmet needs and unvoiced longings—the one who could not ever get her act together—God had seen and known her all along. God had loved her. I could hardly believe it. Part of me wanted to say, "Don't You understand, Lord? There is no good reason to love her. I haven't—why would You? She's of no use to You at all."

That God loves us—*really* loves us—is always a bit more than we can fathom. It comes as an immense surprise. We have never been loved in such a fashion. Who could ever believe that God would look *past* all the special talents, all the helpful deeds, and say, "There, now I've found her"?

God's love is not like any we have ever known because it is offered not to the part of us that performs so well but to our *real self.* This is why His love stuns us. As David

Seamands said, "For it's your real self which God loves and for which Christ died, your real self with all its sins and flaws which He has always known and never stopped loving. Feeling this at gut level gives you courage to face yourself as you truly are."[1] This is the reason that "Just as I Am" is not a song for novitiates. It describes the only way that we can ever really come to God.

One of the most striking places in the Old Testament where this kind of love is pictured is in the book of Hosea. Here, in a wonderful passage in the second chapter, Hosea explains how God lured stubborn Israel into the wilderness. Wildernesses are those places in life where it all begins to fall apart. It is precisely the kind of place where each of us expects to be reprimanded and punished for all those ways we've fallen short. Yet God does the unreasonable thing. "I will allure her, bring her into the wilderness, and *speak kindly to her*," He says (verses 14-15, NASB; emphasis added). There He gave her vineyards and made the valley of "trouble" into a door of hope. This is the picture of what God's love is like: a love that is offered in the places and at the times we least expect it.

The cross is the place where we are known in all our ugliness and shame—and loved. There, on an old Roman cross, hung One whose wounds heal with the salve of an unreasonable love. The cross is the place where we draw our courage to come out of hiding. There we see God's pain somehow mingled with our own. The same vulnerable strength *that comes out of* weakness and dependence on the Father is made available to us.

These are the kind of spiritual realities, though, that have to become deeply personal in order to have any effect on our lives. Frederick Buechner describes one such moment in his life when he felt that God did not just love the world; He loved *him*. He was receiving communion one morning in a small village church where he knew the priest well. As the priest moved nearer, Buechner could hear him intoning the familiar words, "The body of Christ, the Bread of Heaven." Over and over the phrase was repeated.

But when the priest came to him, on an impulse he inserted another word: "The body of Christ, *Freddy*, the Bread of Heaven." There was nothing unusual about the priest knowing his name, Buechner admits. But the effect on *him* was what was extraordinary. It caught him off guard. He says,

> For the first time in my life, maybe, it struck me that when Jesus picked up the bread at his last meal and said, "This is my body which is for you," he was doing it not just in a ritual way . . . but in an unthinkably personal way for every particular man or woman or child who ever existed or someday would exist. Most unthinkable of all: maybe he was doing it for me.[2]

The stark truth of the cross, Buechner writes, is that "we are welcomed not as the solid citizens that our Sunday best suggests we are, but in all our tackiness and tatteredness that nobody in the world knows better than each of us knows it about ourselves—the bitterness and the phoniness and the confusion and the irritability and the prurience and the half-heartedness. The bread of heaven, *Freddy*, of all people."[3]

A character in a children's Christmas book, a little girl named "Awful Abigail," reminds me of how we long for this kind of love. Awful Abigail is the daughter of the owner of the inn where Mary and Joseph sought a room, a "dreadful little girl" who got in everyone's hair. But one night she saw a couple come to the door and sensed something special was astir. Hours later, she set off in search of them. At long last, she saw a light near the manger.

Her search was over. She opened the door and took a few timid steps inside. The story ends by saying that "somehow she knew, a dream had come true, and *Someone who loved her had found her.*"[4]

The paradox of the gospel is that in our search for God we discover He has found us. He looks beyond our pretense and posturing, and He embraces us in our shame, in that state we could only call "awful." We have been at last introduced to a love we could never earn. A love meant to free us from frittering away our lives in pursuit of the ultimate achievement or person to please whose smile makes life worth living. To surrender to that reality is to feel something severed on the inside begin to come back together again. We are loved.

A LOVE THAT MUST BE RISKED

I wish I could bottle the experience of that feeling, the deep understanding that God loves me as I am. Then I could pull it down off the shelf and inhale some whenever my internal supply got low. If only that sense of feeling richly loved was something that could be stored up and saved for a rainy day when nothing was going right.

But feeling secure in that kind of love is something, amazingly enough, that is not meant to be experienced alone. Somehow love has to be risked in relationship in order to be found once again. It is not a commodity to be hoarded. Instead our supply increases as it's given away, as we open ourselves to what we most fear: the potential hurt or rejection of others.

As David Seamands explained in *Healing Grace*, "The kind of honesty and self-knowledge which will bring about lasting changes in our lives almost always requires another person. It is when we disclose our true, private selves to someone else that we fully come to know ourselves for real."[5]

❦

"Maybe it's only my imagination, but I sense that there is distance in our relationship that wasn't there two months ago," Julia said. "I don't know, what do you think, Harriet?"

Julia had to work up the nerve for days to get those words out of her mouth. There, she had finally said them. She couldn't let the awkwardness go on one more day.

Julia and her friend, Harriet, had been close ever since they both moved to Portland nearly five years ago. Their children acted more like cousins than neighbors, so frequently did they go back and forth between the two houses. But not too long ago, Julia and Harriet had gotten in a small, heated discussion about the way Harriet treated a mutual friend. Julia was tempted to back down, as she usually did. She knew if the conversation went much further she'd cry, and then she always heard little voices of admonishment from the past: "Little girls that frown and cry aren't very pretty. They're not pleasant to be around." How well she remembered.

But the conversation had been cut short by Harriet's appointment, so they had parted amicably enough. It was just that ever since, Harriet had grown silent and cold. Julia was tempted to continue to ignore their disagreement, to hope that somehow she could warm the frozen ground between them with kindness and good humor.

It hadn't worked, she had to admit. There was nothing to do but bring the problem out in the open.

❦

Life is full of encounters like this one, small scenes where fear and love vie for supremacy. That is what happens in the world of relationships: As we move toward someone or allow them to move toward us we are led into the center of our own fear.

What exactly is that fear? The Bible indicates this fear is one of death. Not so much physical death as a psychological, emotional kind of nonexistence. It seems as though our soul, the essence of who we are, is at stake. This fear of "death" must be quite real to each of us on a subconscious level—witness the skill and desperation with which we grab defensive masks (a superself) to protect ourselves. We fear others, who appear to have the power to painfully expose the neediness and inadequacy in us. Jesus addressed this fear when He focused the disciples' attention on the gravity of words. He said that to merely call another person a fool was to be guilty of hell.[6] There are ways to "murder" someone that don't require a sword or draw blood. It is possible to "kill" something in a person with a word. And because we sense that possibility, we hide in fearful self-protection.

Yet fear makes slaves of its subjects. It prevents us from ever really being ourselves—and even more, it short-circuits our ability to love someone else genuinely. It siphons off the energy of real love in all the effort it takes to keep our image locked in place.

Here, again, Christ's death speaks directly to the patterns that have kept us in this kind of relational bondage. The writer of Hebrews says that God took on flesh so that He could render the enemy powerless, so that He might "free those who all their lives were held in slavery *by their fear of death*" (2:14-15, emphasis added). The fear of what others can do to us is exactly the slavery, in the context of relationships, that God wants to free us from.

When I was about ten years old, I decided to pick up a black leather Bible that had been tossed in a corner of the living room and try to understand this unfathomable book for myself. I took the book to my room, crawled up on the bed, and began to read. The first place I happened to turn was Psalm 121. Strangely enough, the words made some sense. Especially the last part hit home. I remember running to my father with the verses I had discovered. "Daddy, have you ever seen these words?" I said. "Listen to this." And I began to read.

> The LORD is your keeper;
> The LORD is your shade on your right hand.
> The sun will not smite you by day,
> Nor the moon by night.
> The LORD will protect you from all evil;
> *He will keep your soul.*
> (121:5-7, NASB; emphasis added)

"He will keep my soul." What a beautiful thought that seemed at the time. I imagined God somehow cupping His hands around something He considered precious enough to save, valuable enough to protect.

But as I grew older, I lost that feeling of God's protection—or more accurately, I bargained it away by trying to save myself. I hid in cheap safety behind a maze of superfluous activity and stellar performance until I lost touch with the very soul I was afraid of exposing in the first place.

Now God brought me, once again, back to the first Bible truth I had discovered as a child—only in a deeper and more immediate way. Would I risk letting go of my dependence on the ability to control life by working so hard to appear perfect? Would I risk loving others in the simplicity of who I really was? Would I trust God that He could indeed "keep my soul"?

Those were not easy questions for me to answer. Instinctively, I knew that God was inviting me to walk straight into my fears of failure and inadequacy. I sensed that the chance to taste His love again and again and again would come as I risked my life in relationships where the possibility of brushing up against something that shamed me was ever real.

During those months, a descriptive biblical phrase spoken of Jesus began to wander in and out of my mind, like a little golden strand being woven through a piece of cloth. *"The power of an indestructible life"* was the kind of power that the writer of Hebrews claimed Christ had (7:16). Jesus knew that He could give Himself because He could not be destroyed by anything, even death on a cross. From humility and brokenness would come life. That was the joy before Him—that although He despised the shame of such a death, nothing could ultimately come between Him and His Father.

"The power of an indestructible life"—how those words continue to woo me. They express what each of us longs for and what the death of Christ was meant to secure. God seems to plant our feet on more solid ground by actually inviting us to step into the risky places we most naturally avoid. It seems to be the only way we discover that our soul—our real self—is kept in our Father's invincible care.

The English poet W. B. Yeats late in his life penned words that speak of what it means to discover God's unreasonable love. He wrote,

> But love has pitched his mansion in
> The place of excrement;
> *For nothing can be sole or whole*
> *That has not been rent.*

When we finally realize God's love for us, we are "rent" of our well-crafted defenses. And in that awkward naked-ness, we begin to discover the substance of our soul. It is through wading into this kind of brokenness—rather than running away—that we experience an increasing sense of wholeness and dependence on God.

SUMMING UP

Climbing down off the treadmill of compulsive living is a slow process of coming to understand more about your own internal dynamics. It requires time and thought and the willingness to feel deeply. In this kind of discovery process, it's as though someone shines a flashlight on long-forgotten memories and images in your mind. Your past relationships, the role you may have played in your family—these are some of the clues to the kind of patterns you adopted in life and the reasons for them. Noticing the prerecorded speeches in your thoughts, those inner voices that push you forward, is another.

This kind of process progressively peels back the layers of our self-awareness, beckoning us to venture outside the ivory tower in which we've isolated our authentic soul. Our entrance into that life outside comes at the invitation of One who, as the psalmist said, knows our frame and remembers that we are but dust. God has always seen past our defenses and known us as we are. It is His relentless pursuit of us that gives us the courage to come out of hiding.

The slow metamorphosis that begins to take place in our lives is not the result of more white-knuckled determination and willpower. Change of this sort doesn't come from trying harder. It comes from an altered perception of ourselves, of God, and of others. It comes in small "Aha!" moments, places when we stand outside our immediate experience as an interested observer and realize we are free to choose a different path. A path of grief for what our deception has cost us—and for what it cost the people in our lives as we strove to make them accomplices in the driven life we led. A path of joy, as we discover more "want-tos" than "have-tos," new permission to slow down and ease up. A path of wonder, which intersects with others' lives in meaningful ways.

The last section of this book will explore some of those paths and the joys and the disappointments that come along the way.

NOTES

1. David Seamands, *Healing Grace* (Wheaton, IL: Victor Books, 1989), page 121.
2. Frederick Buechner, "Faith and Fiction," from a collection of essays in the book, *Spiritual Quests* (Boston: Houghton Mifflin, 1988), page 108.
3. Buechner, page 108.
4. Carol Greene, *The Innkeeper's Daughter* (St. Louis: Concordia Publishing House, 1973).
5. Seamands, page 180.
6. Matthew 5:22.

PART · THREE

The Way Change Looks and Feels

CHAPTER TEN

Longings: Making Those Important Inner Connections

All my longings lie open before you, O LORD.
PSALM 38:9

My friend Sarah has just quit her job. We gulp down our morning coffee and hope the waitress will soon bring breakfast. I can tell, as we wait, that Sarah is feeling mildly euphoric. I am curious to know why. Most people feel anything but pleased when a job is over. But not my friend. Relief is written all over her face.

"Why did you quit?" I ask her. "And why do you look so happy?"

From that simple, forthright question the story unfolds. After falling apart in her boss's office one recent Thursday afternoon, Sarah asked to take the next day off and see if she could get herself back together. Surprisingly, her boss agreed.

But by Sunday afternoon, she had done more than get herself together. She had time to think. The last two-and-a-half years had been crazy. Ever since she had taken this job as the executive assistant to a vice president in a manufacturing company, her life had been a whirlwind.

"At first I didn't mind working late and coming in on weekends," she told me. "But there was never a letup, and

I slowly gave up hope there ever would be."

Sarah had gotten caught in the familiar cycle. The more effective she was, the more her boss excelled. The faster he climbed, the more she struggled to keep up. She didn't want to disappoint him. And she kept hoping that one day he would praise her without using the word *but* in the middle of the sentence. Instead of hearing, "That was a great job, Sarah, but next time you need to . . ." Sarah longed to hear, simply, "That was a great job." Period.

Sarah tried to tell her boss that she was feeling burned out, but he could never stop long enough to hear her. She had hoped that, at some point, all her extra work would earn her a bit of rest.

"A month ago when the doctor told me I have an ulcer due to stress, I finally realized that the change in pace would have to come from me," Sarah finished explaining.

I waited a few moments and let her story sink in. We talked some about the kind of job she was looking for now and what she was doing in the meantime. Then I gently put forward my last question.

"What do you think you got out of that arrangement at work?" I said. "What kept you running in place for so long?"

Sarah laid down her muffin on the plate and looked at me strangely. She'd never thought in terms like that. On the surface, it didn't seem that she had gotten *anything* from work but a paycheck and a headache. She felt used.

"I don't know," she replied. "I honestly don't know."

❦

Those were hard questions for me to ask. But I knew that without an answer, Sarah would probably find another equally impossible place to work. She had to know what unmet needs in her own life kept her stuck in overdrive. She had to be able to name the song, so to speak, before she could stop dancing to the fiddle.

Sarah was right on one count in particular, though. The freedom to step off the treadmill has to come from the inside of us. It is so tempting to think, "If my husband would only say . . . if my children were different . . . if work weren't such a hassle . . . *then* I could really make changes." But that is not the case. The off-button exists—but it exists in us.

A variety of *inner movements* hold the key to experiencing a different style of life and relating to others. When I use the words *inner movements*, I do not mean a new list of things to do. Inner movements are contrary to the way that most of us, as over-productive, overdoing women, have lived because they do not describe external behaviors.

An inner movement is connected to a change in perception that naturally elicits new and different ways of doing things. These are changes that you don't make happen as much as you watch them happen.

LONGINGS

Beginning to experience the inner movements of change is intimately connected to our *longings*. Each of us is born with the natural desire to love and be loved and to make a contribution that matters. These are powerful, innate motivations of the human heart. We don't outgrow them. They do not lessen with age. To some extent, we go the whole of our lives with those longings and needs imperfectly met.

It is these unmet longings and needs that fuel the energy of our behavior, especially the energy behind our overdoing. Our odyssey out of the shadows of perfectionism and indispensability is filled with a host of small connections between our longings and our resident fears and everyday choices.

There are many ways to describe those longings, but for our purposes I will choose two. Let's look more closely at them.

The Need to Feel Loved and Wanted

When Sarah's boss would occasionally pull up a chair in her office, loosen his tie, and begin to savor the four o'clock coffee he hoped would give him the energy to work until seven, she knew that she was being included in something special. Something that felt really good. Those were the few moments when he shared his own frustrations and even occasionally asked her advice. The interaction was not romantic, really. What Sarah gained was a tiny drop of the affirmation she craved. And that approval translated into a sense of feeling loved and wanted by an important person in her life—a person she worked until she got an ulcer trying to please.

Each of us longs for reassurance that the significant people in our lives accept us unconditionally and want us around. Rejection or disapproval hurts, and hurts deeply, because it strikes at the core of an innate longing to be loved.

The Need to Feel Our Contribution Matters

The weeks that Sarah spent preparing materials for her boss's company presentations were highlights in her schedule. There was a lot of pressure, but still, she got to see the reward of her work. She knew, and her boss knew, that her efforts more than doubled his effectiveness. To some degree, seeing the fruit of her labor affect corporate policy helped to compensate for his perfectionistic tendencies.

Each of us longs to feel that what we have to offer makes a difference. We want our lives to mean something. On those occasions when we conclude that all our efforts add up to very little, we feel the loss of having significant impact.

It would be easy to conclude that *our longings* get us into trouble. "If only I could find a way not to need I would be okay." That's the inner statement many of us live by. But it never works because our longings are expressions of legitimate needs that don't go away. True spiritual growth makes us only more aware of their presence. The pleasure in a child's face when she is complimented or the pained expression when someone turns away, we recognize as reflections of our own longings. We never grow past our longings to be loved and to feel that our lives matter. Nor should we try.

In fact, our progress in breaking out of patterns of perfectionism and overwork can be measured, in part, by the extent to which our inner voice loses its harsh edge. "Don't need . . . don't want . . . don't ask for," those are the negative messages that must give way to a genuine compassion for ourselves—a compassion that reflects the way God feels toward us. He is the One, after all, who instilled in us the need to be loved and to matter. Those longings form the path from our heart to His. They are the source of our spiritual passion.

You can see evidence of this kind of intensity of desire when you read many of the psalms. "My soul is consumed with longing for your laws. . . . My soul faints with longing for your salvation," writes the author of Psalm 119 (verses 20,81). There is almost a note of desperation in his voice. These are the words of someone who knows that what his heart longs for is so infinite that only God is enough to satisfy his soul.

"Only God. . . ." What is it about those words that is so hard to bear, sometimes? Perhaps because they remind us that the best this life can offer is so limited only God can really meet the deepest stirrings of our hearts. Not until we are in His eternal presence will the ache go away.

"Inconsolable longings"—that's the phrase C. S. Lewis used to describe this ache, because no matter what we get in this life—a new dress, a sincere compliment, or a warm hug—it will soothe the pain only temporarily. It always returns as an inner guide that leads us toward Home. What God asks of us now is that we live in hopeful expectancy. Someday every longing of our hearts will be met, and we will never again feel like a child with her school bags packed, making daisy chains by the curb, waiting for a parent to come.

Acknowledging the gap between need and reality can lead to hope and not despair. It is a relief to accept the truth: No amount of hard work or great performance will bring that final sense of inner completeness and fulfillment you've searched for. There is no magic secret that, once discovered, will make the ache forever go away. Our longings are not an indication of something wrong, but "of something more profoundly right than we could ever dream of."[1]

Recognizing that gap between your longings and your experience also sensitizes you to those moments, those small encounters that touch you on a deep emotional level. It lets you savor their sweetness all the more.

My husband travels frequently and his absence gives me plenty of time to recognize my "unmet longings." A few summers ago, he left for a month overseas, after which the children and I would join him for another month in Singapore. While he was gone, the house slowly fell apart. Major appliances broke down. Large bills came due. The workmen finishing our kitchen were a month behind schedule. One morning a few days before we were scheduled to join him, it all came to a head. I woke up feeling utterly overwhelmed.

Before long, tears began to pour down my cheeks, steady profuse tears that refused to stop. And right in the middle of it all, a curious thought popped into my head: *Paula, why have you always kept moments such as these to yourself? Why do you just stuff it and go on?*

Suddenly I knew the next step to take. I picked up the phone and did something I had never done before. "Do you have a half hour where I could come over and just talk this out?" I asked a good friend. In a few minutes, there I was on her back porch pouring out my tale.

I talked and cried while my friend just listened, handing me one tissue after another. She gave me something I had always desired but rarely, if ever, experienced. She permitted me to know the relief of being able to fall apart without feeling ashamed. She let me need another person's encouragement, someone "with skin on," who could empathize without thinking she had to fix my problem.

My normal reaction to the stress of such a month would have been to wash my tears, if there were any, down the bathroom sink. I would have buried my need in a bigger effort to get ready for the trip. But because I was able to recognize what I longed for, and the legitimacy of that longing, I could really appreciate the sense of being received by a friend. I could share the situation with someone and thereby lessen the load.

Acknowledging our longings opens us to the bittersweet joy of having them occasionally met in deep ways. Those experiences are sweet because they touch us where we really live. And they are "bitter" because they can't be engineered or forced, and there is no guarantee when they will happen again.

RELEASING OUR GRIP

Those of us who are plagued with the tendency to do too much live with longings that are, for the most part, unacknowledged and unmet.

The reality of living with unmet longings can lead us to deny their existence, to our great detriment. It is easier to pretend we don't care and get busy—real busy—with the demands of a big, important distraction. Betty Friedan once remarked that she preferred to start the feminist movement rather than face the pain and unmet needs in her own life. But longings, left unacknowledged, are still operative. In fact, they gain intensity and an edge of desperation as we deny their presence. This is part of what gives the out-of-control, choiceless, compulsive quality to our lives.

Like Sarah, we get caught in a situation that offers some slim thread of misbegotten hope for meeting needs we cannot consciously acknowledge. Or even when we may be quite aware of our longings, we misdirect our efforts toward their fulfillment. We become prisoners of longings we deny. And then, as the Apostle Paul said, we end up doing the things we hate—or instead, doing too much of the things we love.

Miriam's weekend ritual always included a careful perusal of the *Philadelphia Dispatch.* But news and commentary were not her real concern. Miriam was a first-class shopper. If a good sale was within twenty-five miles, she was usually there.

Her friends used to joke that if they wanted to visit with her they'd have to bring a thermos and pour two cups of coffee by a clothes rack in a department store. Her husband often groaned when he saw the latest load of stuff coming in the front door. "I'm going to have to cut up our charge cards," he would threaten. Miriam, herself, half-resented the expenditure of energy that shopping required. But, given a few hours of leisure time, her car usually headed for the nearest mall, as if on automatic pilot.

> Clothes were her biggest weakness. She bought clothes she didn't need and even some she never wore. Some magic must take place in the dressing room of a good women's dress shop, Miriam decided. Some hidden tilt to the mirrors. Her hips looked smaller; the dark rings under her eyes seemed to fade. Was it the lighting, perhaps? Miriam only knew that standing there in a new dress, she felt young again—young and pretty.
>
> And for Miriam, looking pretty was only a breath away from feeling loved.

❦

Longings that go unacknowledged, as we have said, grow in intensity. They harden into demands. In the process, it feels as though we lose our ability to choose. Like Miriam, we're heading back to the mall (or taking dinner to a friend or rewriting an already good report) even when it's not terribly necessary. Even when we don't want to. But somehow, without our conscious awareness, a particular activity has become enmeshed with the hope of feeling loved or significant, powerful or affirmed or needed. We begin to fill in the gap between desire and fulfillment with some form of driven behavior. And then we're hooked.

Once this process gains enough momentum, it takes on a life of its own. Whatever we have to do to recapture or prolong that special feeling, we will do. After a while, we have no real idea what is driving us. The connection between an unmet longing and a present choice has become obscured. We know only that the cost to ourselves and others seems more justifiable. Our grip tightens around a bright, shiny thing with the promise of relief from pain or the promise of a fulfilled longing. We're trapped.

An appropriate analogy for how this happens is found in the way that raccoons are caught and carried off from their natural, free habitat. All that is required is a special trap with a small opening on one end and a bright, shiny object (literally) on the other. Once the raccoon reaches in and grasps what he wants, he balls his little paw into a fist. If he tries to pull it out, sharp, pointed nails inside the trap jab his fist and he stays put. He stays put for hours. He sits there with his paw gripped around that bright, shiny thing even when there's food nearby to rid him of his hunger.

His freedom is not all that difficult to secure. If he would only release his grip around the shiny object, he could pull out his paw and be on his way. He could go free.

This is much like the way a woman is caught in the trap of any driven activity, whether it's food or work or leading Bible studies. In some way her inner grip tightens, and it all becomes do or die. "I ought to . . . I should . . . I must." She continues because of where her hope lies. When false hope gets tangled inseparably with longings, then a pernicious lie takes root.

We must continue, we must hold on to the shiny thing, because *this is where our life is.* The object of our desire, then, gets confused. It appears, for all the world, to be the next promotion or others' applause or something that brings a fleeting feeling of importance.

There is an incredibly deceptive nature to any kind of "obsession" because a subtle form of idolatry lies at its core. We become deceived into thinking that our life, our well-being, depends on a false god—such as working harder, pleasing people, or looking thinner. The prophet Isaiah described this kind of internal deception with these words: "He feeds on ashes, a deluded heart misleads him; *he cannot save himself, or say, 'Is not this thing in my right hand a lie?'"* (44:20, emphasis added). Like Miriam, whose car automatically heads for the mall, we become blind to the realities that enslave us.

Slavery of this sort breeds on fear. Fear that if we don't perform or don't please we will lose our place in the scheme of things. This inner grip of control is much like the raccoon's tightly balled fist: only what we grasp is whatever looks like "life" to us. Frozen in our sculpted patterns of overdoing, a great deal of real life passes us by in a host of small moments and close encounters we either don't recognize and appreciate or we run from out of fear. Like the raccoon, we merely subsist, oblivious to the possibilities around us.

During the months when I was first wading into a different way of being, I remember pausing one afternoon to jump rope with Allison on the sidewalk outside our home. All of a sudden we both tripped, and before I knew it, we had tumbled into a pile of freshly cut grass. Neither of us made any move to get up right away. We just lay there together for a few minutes, laughing at the sheer silliness of it all.

Why haven't I done this more? I found myself thinking. *What have I been missing all these years?* I realized then that probably hundreds of moments like this had been right under my nose all the time. Moments I never stopped long enough to enjoy because I was so intent on reaching my goals.

Notice that what would free the raccoon is the act of *letting go*. That phrase describes one of the very first inner movements that marks the recovery of a woman who does too much. *Letting go* is a phrase she returns to many times.

What does it mean to let go? "Letting go is like releasing a tight spring at the core of yourself, one that you've spent your whole life winding and maintaining," according to author Sue Monk Kidd.[2] Letting go is about relinquishment, not trying harder, waiting, letting things be. It is almost as simple as it sounds. For women who have spent our lives forging ahead, its chief difficulty is that it's just so contrary to what we've known.

This brings to mind an analogy. Most of us have lived like the inexperienced ranching woman out west who sat atop her buggy, holding the reins of her horses just so, until something spooked the horses and they took off. Onlookers yelled to her, "Let go! Let go of the reins!" But she was so afraid, she couldn't. The team of horses finally broke away from the buggy, dragging her limp and lifeless behind them.

I use that illustration because letting go is about dropping the reins, releasing control. It is a spiritual act in that it takes place on the inside. Letting go means that we are beginning to see that the shiny thing of perfectionism, in whatever form it appears, holds no life for us. Letting go is a transforming act of surrender and repentance that leads us to God.

One woman expressed the feeling this way: "I see myself on the outer edge of a cliff—part of me hanging on for dear life to my old ways of managing my fear of being out of control, the other part of me wanting so much to just let go of those outworn strategies and tumble into what somewhere deep inside me I know will be the tenderness of God's hand."

What we let go of is not our longings—our desire to love and be loved and to live a life that matters—but our *demand*, the compulsive activity that deceitfully promises, while actually stealing our life.

FACING THE GAP

In the book of Joel, the prophet uses a particular phrase to describe what it meant for Israel to return to the Lord: "*Rend your heart and not your garments*" (2:13). These were Joel's words. And they can be applied as well to the whole phenomenon of what it means to experience change that is more than skin deep.

If we long for freedom from the treadmill, we have to deal with our hearts, with the source of our affections and attachments. Change begins with inner movements like letting go—letting go of what we have used to control our life, to hide from relationship, to play it safe. It begins in experiencing more of our true longings and recognizing some of the misplaced hopes and prodigal paths we've followed to satisfy them.

While that sounds simple enough, there is both a quality of beauty and of fierceness to the process.[3]

It is beautiful because experiencing our longings always brings us back to God. It's the homecoming of a child who senses her Father's pleasure in her return and finds in His smile a small measure of the freedom that enables love.

But it is fierce as well. Letting go brings us squarely into the center of the gap between our desires and present, everyday reality. It is fierce because that entails all sorts of risks and enduring losses, which are very real. It is fierce because it propels us out of our comfortable patterns of working harder and helping more into places that feel awkward and empty and new.

When we encounter this "emptiness," this gap between our true desires and our immediate experience, a mild or raging panic will tempt us to return to our tried-and-true ways of coping. Or we may find ourselves substituting a new compulsive behavior for the abandoned one, as when a recovering alcoholic turns to smoking.

"Although this emptiness is really freedom, it is so unconditioned that it feels strange, sometimes even horrible," admits Gerald May in his book *Addiction and Grace.* "If we were willing for a deeper transformation of desire, we would have to try to make friends with the spaciousness; we would need to appreciate it as openness to God."[4]

The difference between "peak performers" and "pace addicts," research confirms, is that the peak performer acquires this ability to stand back, reflect, and reconsider, whereas the pace addict is forever preoccupied with the frenzy of the moment. She can't live with the void. She abhors the absence of emotional intoxication and the false sense of omnipotence that doing too much brings. She becomes addicted to an artificial high that leaves her flat and despairing, much like a sugared pastry deadens one's appreciation for a piece of good fruit.

Facing the gap between what you long for and what you are experiencing means different things to different women. It varies with our own particular circumstances and personal struggles.

Sarah is in the middle of learning a new job. But she is also learning what it's like to work hard and yet stop before she nears exhaustion. She is facing the risks of living within her limits, even when it means she may receive less of the accolades she longs for. In the process, she is able to take up a few hobbies she never had time for, like gardening and photography.

Change for Miriam, on the other hand, means that she's starting to wear more of the clothes that already hang in her closet. She is letting go of the feeling of being "special" that she connected only with looking pretty in something new. Other parts of her personality are beginning to bloom. She is taking a class at a local community college. Her friends are finding that they can actually enjoy a relaxed conversation with her.

Kay, the singer-turned-homemaker in chapter 5, is taking most of the singing opportunities that come her way. But she is confronting her inadequacies by choosing a few rooms in her house to redecorate in some way that really interests her. She is learning to relate to her mother-in-law without measuring herself by another woman's standards.

And Julie, the indispensable woman in chapter 4, is beginning to explore the new territory of what it means to offer herself in relationships—sexually with her husband, and through her own needs and desires with her friends. She is discovering the freedom to enjoy passion and pleasure.

In some way, the strides that each of these women has made have all entailed their willingness to let go of old habit patterns and enter the space that comes with newness. They confronted old inadequacies and chose not to run away. They accepted that initial empty feeling without rushing to fill the void. In Gerald May's words, they "made friends with the spaciousness," by refusing either to deny their longings or demand their immediate fulfillment.

In my own life over the last three years, I chart my course in small increments, tiny inner shifts that are often more noticeable to me than to others. But I can tell the difference. What I notice, first, is that a small scene will open up before me in which I realize I am not a passive participant. I have a choice. I am not frozen mindlessly in the same old pattern.

I think of one occasion, a few years ago, when my husband and I had flown to Houston. We were both excited about our trip, but I was also drained from the effort it took to organize for our children while we were gone. A friend picked us up at the airport for the thirty-minute trip into the city.

Normally, I am the queen of small talk. Stacy, my husband, is more reserved and, in the tradition of German men, speaks when he has something vital to say. Over the years I have almost unconsciously grown used to filling in the spaces of conversation. On this particular day, though, as I was getting ready to "do my usual," I realized that I could let the men carry on as if I were hardly present. It was possible. I could, if I so chose, just sit back and relax.

At first I braced myself for the awkward pauses, the lapses in conversation that I would normally have filled. But I hung on, and by the end of the trip, I had learned a small, much-needed lesson.

These two men, like so many people in my life, were perfectly capable of handling things on their own. The outcome didn't rest on me nearly as much as I thought! It wasn't the conversation the three of us would have had—but it was good enough. Rather than "filling in the gap" I was able to let it be. And what grew in me, in the process, was a measure of respect and gratitude and pure pleasure at being able to let go and rely on someone else. I breathed a sigh of relief.

LOVING OUR LONGINGS

This is just one small incident out of the seemingly hundreds of others that make up real-life change for anyone. What shifts inside of you, among many things, is your definition of strength. Instead of seeing yourself as the "strong one" who must fill what is lacking, you gain an ability to wait on the strength of another.

What happens, though, when a legitimate longing is disappointed? What happens when you take a risk, you let go of your need to control the outcome, you resist the urge to fill in the gap, and your fear is realized? The project isn't as successful as it might have been. Your husband doesn't listen when you cry. Your friend is upset that you aren't as available as you once were.

These are the times when we are most likely to revert to our old patterns of relating. This is the place in the cycle where we most easily derail. When our longings are not met or our efforts to change are not well-received, it's easy to conclude mistakenly, "There must be something wrong with me. I should never have wanted a word of praise, a shoulder to lean on, a friend who offered a reciprocal relationship in the first place. I should never have *wanted* anything."

If we aren't careful, we will bury our longings once again, sever our feelings and desires, and get back to life as it has always been. What will give us the willingness to say "yes" to our longings even in the face of disappointment?

The tiny tastes of freedom we've experienced (like my sigh of relief in the back seat) give us the courage to continue to risk new life. What keeps us going forward is the sure knowledge that our longings will carry us into genuine relationships where we love with a much fuller heart. Our longings will lead us into places of genuine repentance and true choices. Our longings will return us to the Lord as the One who truly satisfies.

Gerald May's words about longings give the best summary:

> To live as a child of God is to live with love and hope and growth, but it is also to live with longing, with aching for a fullness of love that is never quite within our grasp. To claim our rightful place in destiny, we must not only accept and claim the sweetly painful incompleteness within ourselves, but also affirm it with all our hearts. To state it directly, we must come to love our longing.[5]

In the next chapter, we will take a closer look at the way our longings for relationship affect the overall fabric of our lives.

NOTES
1. Dr. Gerald May, *Addiction and Grace* (San Francisco: Harper & Row, 1988), page 180.
2. Sue Monk Kidd, *When the Heart Waits* (San Francisco: Harper & Row, 1990), page 114.
3. May, page 96.
4. May, page 146
5. May, pages 179-180.

CHAPTER ELEVEN

Relationships: Enjoying Intimate Moments

Hope does not disappoint us,
because God has poured out his love
into our hearts by the Holy Spirit,
whom he has given us.
ROMANS 5:5

Last summer our son, Brady, got his first camera. For a while, he carried around his small instamatic every day, letting it hang loosely at his side until he found a shot he considered worthy of preserving with a picture.

When his friend Adam came from Colorado for a visit, we all piled into the car and headed for a few days on the North Carolina coast. Now here was a field day full of possible photographs! Every time I turned around, there was Brady snapping a picture of the Atlantic Ocean. Brady photographing the fishing pier. Brady aiming his camera at a big sand dune.

All of a sudden it hit me. What would a photograph of the ocean mean to Brady six months from now? This sand dune, as spectacular as it was to see it in person, wouldn't bring nearly as much pleasure once it became part of his picture album.

"Brady, honey, you've got to get some *people* in your pictures," I said. "Here, let me take one of you and Adam jumping the waves."

Brady didn't see that, before long, all that had seemed

so big and important in this scene would pale in his memory. The real treasure eventually would be the part easiest to overlook now. Some day what he'd really remember would be a day at the beach with his sister and Adam.

I realized that, in a small way, I was watching a metaphor of my life. This was the way I'd lived much of the time over the years. As a woman on the go, I've been guilty of focusing on events, achievements, and tasks as though they were the important things. I've seen my life like a picture album chock-full of demands on my time and energy. And what I have missed too often has been of the most value: relationships.

Friendships, intimacy, a sense of real connection to other people—this is what is often absent from the landscape of our lives. This is part of the void we've filled with work, duty, caretaking, and achievement. And this is, in many cases, what is necessary to restore balance and sanity to the overall picture.

It's not that there aren't plenty of people around us— there are. It's just that, even in the midst of being surrounded with others, there can be a scarcity of real relationships: of friendships that are marked by reciprocity; of affinity that has little to do with position and status; of intimacy that comes with a sharing of hearts, as well as minds. Our busyness, our helpfulness, our I-can-do-it-myself attitude—too often these things have kept others at arm's length, and we remain lonely and untouched as women.

Relationships are important for another reason, too. Because our wounds have taken place in the context of relationships with others, our healing must also. Intimacy with others is the one sure antidote to self-sufficiency and independence.

For this reason, especially, our progress as women who do too much can almost be measured in terms of our openness to genuine relationships.

SO CLOSE . . . AND YET SO FAR

"After an acquaintance of ten minutes many women will exchange confidences that a man would not reveal to a lifelong friend," writes the American historian Page Smith.[1] As women we are fed and personally nourished by our relationships. Yet there is a dynamic that undercuts this potential in the lives of women who are given to overdoing. Even when our lives are filled with people, often we feel lonely and emotionally isolated.

Two patterns of relating, in particular, prevent us from experiencing intimacy with others—patterns that keep others "close," and yet far away.

Caretaking

Perhaps we could say that caretaking, in its simplest form, is just too much of a good thing. Caretaking is the mutation of a woman's ability to nurture and protect and help. It's a strength carried to extremes. It moves subtly from nurturing to "smothering," from giving to manipulating.

The caretaker's help or advice, her baked casserole or unexpected present is motivated by her own need to guarantee a relationship of some sort. She "loans" her love, hoping against hope to receive in kind.[2] What drives her is the shame of being left alone and the fear of being separate. For this reason, caretaking is a type of giving that often feels "sticky" to the person on the other end. It feels like coercion.

What makes caretaking a threat to a genuine relationship is the absence of freedom. Life-giving relationships are fluid and changeable; they resist guarantees. That's what makes them at once so *precious* and so *tenuous*. Real love can always be refused. There is freedom in both parties to come and go; there is freedom to grow. In trying to grasp people tightly, we often lose them. Thus the woman whose relationships are marked by caretaking often vacillates between two extremes: people who have grown dependent on her, and those who have turned away. In neither case does she herself feel loved or experience the pleasure of loving others with their freedom intact.

Performing

While the caretaker "pursues" relationship to an extreme, the performer "distances" herself out of fear. Often in a relationship, she assumes the role of a coach or a manager. She can rarely let herself be shoulder to shoulder with the next person as simply a friend or sister or coworker. That is getting too close for comfort. The performing woman must find a way to be on top in a relationship in order to maintain her distance. She may be lonely—but at least she's safe.

Those around her tend to feel dwarfed by her presence. Her over-productivity, her drive to perform, leaves them no room to feel needed or appreciated. In fact, they often grow more incapacitated in a kind of "learned helplessness" that fosters resentment. They get tired of looking klutzy and inadequate beside the star performer. And the more incapable they appear, the harder performance-oriented women work in order to make up the perceived deficit.

In the process, the performer is substituting a feeling of competence and hoped-for admiration for intimacy in her closest relationships. She is intent on proving herself. There is no way to have a genuine relationship that touches her deeply—and allows others to be touched by her—until she relaxes her guard.

LIFE-GIVING RELATIONSHIPS

So relationships, then, are central. The ones that are genuine have a mysterious capacity to counteract our tendency to do too much. They channel our energy in positive directions. They make us feel alive. But relationships—the genuine, life-giving kind—are also hard to come by.

A healthy relationship is made up of two currents that ebb and flow, depending on the need of the moment. Those two "currents" are, simply, *giving* and *receiving*. Those words mark the invisible inner movements that have to take place on the inside of us if we are to experience close connections with others.

ॐ

Real Receiving

Nancy poured more cream in her coffee and reached for a spoon. "Would you like some?" she looked up at Melissa just long enough to ask. The ice had formed tiny delicate rivulets on the windowpane behind Melissa's head. It was a relief, a pleasant surprise, to be the only ones in the teachers' lounge late on this winter Tuesday.

"You were telling me about your plans to go to graduate school," Nancy heard Melissa prompting her.

"Yeah, that's what I'm thinking, anyway. It seems like the most logical thing to do next year. Ted has decided that he wants to go to Chicago to live with his dad. I'm going to have a lot of time on my hands," Nancy replied evenly.

There, that was the easiest way to say the awful truth. Melissa already knew about Nancy's divorce. They had, on occasion, even exchanged advice about how to make it on a teacher's salary and raise a teenager. But this was the first time Nancy had told anyone the news about her son. She was having trouble accepting the prospect of Ted being gone.

Melissa looked up from her steaming cup and watched Nancy for a long moment. "I bet that is really hard," she said. "I mean—this thing of Ted wanting to live in Chicago with his dad."

Yeah, it's a killer, all right, Nancy thought silently. Part of her ached to let Melissa know how hard it really was. She could almost feel the load lighten at the prospect of sharing it with someone, even for a few minutes

Nancy took a deep breath and began to tell her friend how it all came about.

❦

When we gather the courage to crack the door an inch or two and allow another person to enter the spot where we are really living, we begin to learn what it is to receive in relationships.

Receiving . . . that's the hard part for women who do too much. We are much better at "giving." But developing a true sense of receptivity is exactly what we need. It means that we have relaxed on the inside and let down our guard. We are present in the immediate moment with another human being. Receptivity implies emotional openness, not only to what we have to give another but to the friendship or support or advice that's being offered to us. Like Nancy, if we are open we find a multitude of tiny moments that are, in themselves, little crossroads. We can choose to receive something from the person we are with—rather than just skirt on by superficially.

Having been married for almost twenty years to a man in full-time Christian ministry, I understand what it means to be on the "giving" end of relationships. That's what ministry traditionally means: giving. You teach and counsel and serve, and in many minds, it feels wrong to ask for anything in return. The whole principle of receptivity in relationships was one I had almost overlooked completely.

But during that summer of depression, I found myself telling Stacy that I felt as though I were having "an allergic reaction to being in ministry," one I didn't understand. I felt depleted, as though seeing one more person who might possibly need or want something from me would cause me to break out in hives. I had nothing more to give. In that state of classic burnout, I discovered the missing part of the whole equation: I had needs—and plenty of them—myself.

Any measure of true receptivity is possible only when we begin to acknowledge our own neediness. That acknowledgment is the willing exposure of our own needs and fears and inadequacies, not in a demanding way, but in an open, receptive one. We have to let go of our superwoman image and take our place among the mooing herd.

Receptivity is the willingness to acknowledge our own neediness and permit another person to touch our lives. It's a legitimate part of being human—of following in the footsteps of One who created the heavens with His fingertips and yet, when He became a man, quite willingly asked His friends to stay awake with Him while He prayed in the garden.

If we've spent most of our lives trying to be strong, capable women, admitting our own needs and limitations comes hard. It flies in the face of self-sufficiency. Yet a part of our soul practically craves strength, not because we don't legitimately have our own, but because we long to relax and rely on someone besides ourselves for a change. Unless we are in touch with the part of us that *needs* something from others, we remain isolated in lonely ghettos with doors that have been locked from the inside.

The opportunity to be responsive to the initiatives of

others comes packaged in many different forms, ways that are easy to overlook as long as you are determined to be the strong one.

I remember one long-distance phone conversation with Stacy where this became clear to me. I had come to Raleigh as a scout to spend a week looking for a house to buy. By the end of that time, both the realtor and I were exhausted. The housing market was at least 30 percent more expensive than the one we were leaving in Colorado. There were a couple of possible options, but nothing to get excited about. By the end of the week, all I really wanted to do was get on a plane and go home.

When Stacy called, I was a bundle of indecision. "You really shouldn't come out here, honey," I told him. "All these houses are running together in my mind. I'm too tired to make a good choice."

"Paula, you don't have to take this on all by yourself," Stacy corrected me. "I'm going to use this extra ticket and fly there tomorrow. We can wade through what you've found together."

His words rang in my ears. *"You don't have to take this on all by yourself."* Oh, yes. I was not required to go through life carrying every weight on my shoulders. I needed someone else's help. And in this instance, I most particularly needed Stacy's help. Relying on him was not a luxury. It was, in this case, the way things were meant to be.

Facing your own neediness has special bearing on your relationships to men. When you are aware of your own needs, an inner sentinel inside you keeps watch, instinctively attuned to the peculiar strength that men have to offer—even if they themselves are not yet aware of it. In this way, you are freed from the trap of copying men and trying to emulate their ways. As a woman, you need what they alone can give. As Dr. Toni Grant explained, "Relating to a man as a woman means allowing oneself to feel soft once again, surrendering to a strength which is uniquely male and permitting oneself to feel pleasure from it."[3]

This kind of "surrender" is anything but a sign of weakness in women. On the contrary, it requires enormous strength and courage for us to let go of some of the control.

Women receive from other women in a special way, as well. There is something richly invigorating in the way that women meet each other—so quickly sometimes—on an emotional plane. That deep intuitive sense of being understood, often without words, is what women are uniquely able to give and receive from each other.

The strange paradox of receiving from another person is that often your receptivity is your greatest gift. When you need someone, you invite that person to actualize his or her strength. It's a way of really *seeing* someone, of saying either in words or actions that what that person has to contribute is something you consider important. It may not be spectacular; it may be obscured from view under layers of bravado or insecurity. But it's there, and your need is the cause that calls it forth. In more instances than you realize, your need is something of a gift.

When our relationships are one-sided and we are forever on the giving end, we effectively shut others out of our lives. Their compliments fall on deaf ears. Their offers to help are shrugged off. Their opinion is discounted. Not being willing to receive makes others feel foolish and inadequate around us. It denies them a pleasure that should be theirs. Without our realizing it, our lack of responsiveness says, "I won't let you matter to me. I won't let you get that close." At its heart, lack of receptivity is a deep-seated form of selfishness.

In the world of relationships, the principle of receptivity is the one most easily overlooked. Yet, it's such an important part of the glue that bonds us together. For those of us who have spent our lives forging ahead and giving out, being able to receive opens a whole new world. It certainly has for me, anyway. I think of it as an emotional way of moving over and making room for someone else. It takes my eyes off myself and saves me from fruitless comparisons. The questions of who's better and who's ahead begin to fade in the light of deeper ones: How can I draw out the best this person has to give? How can I receive and enjoy people for who they really are?

Real Giving

"Sally, would you take a few minutes to go over this draft of my speech next week?" her husband, John, asked casually. He laid the text on her nightstand. "It needs the touch of a good English teacher."

Sally smiled and said she would, but inside she cringed. It wasn't that she really minded taking out her red teacher's pen and correcting her husband's punctuation. She knew, from experience over the years, what she could expect to see on those pieces of paper. What was hard for her was all that those pages represented.

When Sally added her finishing touches and corrected John's grammar she was reminded how very different they were as two individuals. For all his success in the business world, he was an old farm boy at heart. Candor and straightforward simplicity—those were his strengths. No one would ever accuse him of being an intellectual. John was a world away from Sally's private school upbringing. And every time she read one of his speeches, she was painfully reminded of that fact.

Sally caught the uneasiness with which John had laid his speech on her nightstand. In the past, her "corrections" had been the occasions for heated arguments. John could feel that beneath the red ink lay her steady effort to shape him into something he knew he wasn't and didn't want to be. Yet he needed her help. It was as simple as that.

❦

If you think of "giving" in a relationship as your movement toward another person, then that would seem to be the part of the equation with which we are most familiar. But what constitutes real giving deserves a second glance.

"For God so loved the world that He *gave*. . . ." So begins one of the most-quoted verses in the Gospel of John. That's what characterizes God. He made the first move toward us; His was a love that gave. If we take a deeper look at what His giving to us was like, we discover the first principle of genuine giving in a relationship: His love was offered with an absence of strings attached. He moved toward us in a way that did not overpower our freedom to respond to Him. As Frederick Buechner once observed, "He comes in a way that we can always turn Him down."[4]

Real giving in any relationship is like this. It doesn't force itself on another, and most importantly, it gives up the notion of control. That's the hidden dynamic in Sally's help that made John instinctively wary. He needed her expertise, but he also felt the sting of her coaching and her critique. Sally's "giving" was tainted by her own desperate need to script John into the man she wished he was. Her giving came with the price tag of control.

Offering something freely to another person is almost

impossible as long as our deepest concern is self-directed. No matter how good our efforts may appear, such giving has little to do with the other person. We are giving in order to get: to win someone's approval, to straighten the person out, to ensure love in return. And others know the giving is not about them; it's about us.

That's what makes genuine caring more of a challenge than it first appears. We are able to give without strings attached only as we find some measure of our own safety and significance in the grace of God. We are able to love, as the Apostle John said, because we have been loved by God first.[5]

The joy that comes in this kind of giving is that we are able to give without an expectation of reward, other than the pure, intrinsic pleasure of knowing we are contributing some real aspect of who we are to another. We offer ourselves—our perspective or sympathy or home-cooked meal or whatever—with an open hand, an open heart.

I watched this take place in a friend's life recently. As a lay counselor, she had been invited to a meeting to help critique a new counseling program. When she arrived, she realized she was the only woman in a room full of men, most with Ph.D.'s. To further complicate matters, within ten minutes she also realized she was the only person present who had real reservations about the proposed program. She was strongly tempted to remain silent. *No, she thought, I've worked with people for ten years. I have valid thoughts to offer this group.* The joy came in being able to share her insights without requiring the group to follow her advice or validate the worth of her perception. Her own identity was not on the line.

Finally, real giving springs from some enlightened knowledge of your true capabilities. In other words, you can offer another only what you genuinely have to give. And while it's easy to fall into the trap of trying to be everything to everybody, becoming a jack of all trades and master of none, it won't work over the long haul. Perhaps you're gifted at hospitality or organization. Or maybe your speciality is financial planning or preparing a motivating speech or being a perceptive listener. But chances are, you do not possess all of the above. The truth is, you can offer only what you've been equipped to give—anything else is usually not much of a gift. Such overextended effort would often be better left un-given.

FREE TO LOVE

As we move away from our patterns of compulsive living, new reservoirs of energy become available to the cause of loving others. This is the proper place for willpower and strength. Gerald May wrote, "We bring our intention, our efforts, our strength, and all else that we can muster to the cause of love."[6]

Henri Nouwen, in his book about intimacy and joy, says that in life-giving relationships we hold another person much like someone would hold a wounded bird.[7] If we clasp the other person too tightly, we squeeze the life out of the relationship. And if we hold on too loosely, the relationship flounders. Instead, what we must offer each other, he says, is a warm incubating space—as though our hands were gently cupped—a free space that offers room to maneuver, room to grow. In that free place a genuine sense of intimacy and connection to another can be experienced.

The experience of intimacy, in actuality, takes place in small unpredictable moments that add up, over time, to a close relationship. No matter what words or images we choose to describe "intimacy," those kinds of moments resist any effort to control them. We can't make them happen. They come on their own timetable, in brief snatches, with no promise that they will return again. All moments of feeling connected to someone hold this in common: The most we can do is to be open to receive them. As women, we are uniquely equipped to savor and appreciate those encounters.

Whether someone is male or female, this quality of remaining open leaves us all in such a vulnerable position. It means our defenses are down. And because of that, we will come to experience more of the pleasure of enjoying relationships than we have known. But the other side of the coin is true as well. We will be more aware of loneliness and rejection—those painful realities that we shielded ourselves from in the past with hard work and efforts to please. The very word *vulnerability* means "able to be wounded." Intense pleasure and very real pain inherently come with the territory of loving and being loved.

Learning to love requires our willingness to take risks in relationships. Simply put, we risk being hurt. And as we risk, we build up layers of trust in relationships. But the risking itself never gets easy. As Gerald May said,

> Because real risking in faith can occur only in those areas of life where we feel most impoverished and vulnerable, it never becomes something we are really comfortable with. . . . Each choice remains difficult; what really becomes conditioned in this process is simply our willingness and readiness to take the risks of faith. They never stop feeling like risks.[8]

Ultimately, our greatest comfort is the reality that God "has poured out his love into our hearts," just as Paul stated in Romans 5:5. If the resources were purely our own, we'd be in trouble. But as it is, we are the mediators of His love, and the freer we are of our own worn-out strategies for life, the better able we are to receive that love and pass it on to someone else. In the final analysis, we have been included in the love of the Father and the Son and the Holy Spirit—an intimacy where honor, deference, and respect abound. An intimacy where each is separate and yet integrally part of the whole.

Here in this, the true Source of love, we know that when we run out of a temporary supply, we are invited to return for more.

NOTES
1. Page Smith, as quoted in *Friendship* (Philadelphia: Running Press, 1989), page 23.
2. Dr. John Townsend, *Hiding from Love* (Colorado Springs: NavPress, 1991), page 223.
3. Dr. Toni Grant, *Being a Woman* (New York: Avon Books, 1988), page 163.
4. Frederick Buechner, as quoted by Philip Yancey, *Disappointment with God* (Grand Rapids: Zondervan, 1988), page 106.
5. 1 John 4:19.
6. Dr. Gerald May, *Addiction and Grace* (San Francisco: Harper & Row, 1988), page 175.
7. Henri Nouwen, *Lifesigns* (New York: Seabury, 1981), pages 13-14.
8. May, pages 127-130.

CHAPTER TWELVE

Embracing the Journey: Cultivating a Spirit of Adventure

*Blessed are those whose strength is in you,
who have set their hearts on pilgrimage.*
PSALM 84:5

Much of the initial understanding about my own driven approach to life took place during the last year that we lived in Colorado. As we packed up to move to North Carolina, I felt as though I was making a clean break. I had hopes that a new me was hopping into the moving van.

But we were moving back to the South, to the land of moonlight and magnolias where I grew up, and I had forgotten what that meant. This was the place where I first refined my natural tendency to be a woman who does too much. The mandate to be picture perfect, carefully pressed, and perpetually pleasant is simply assumed in these parts, as though it came ready-made in the local water supply.

I had thought after fifteen years in the Midwest I would be immune to that pull. But I discovered I was not.

After only a few months, the old pressure was back. I felt the pressing weight of all sorts of external expectations. Before long, I was back at my old ways again—pushing too hard, stuffing my feelings, polishing an outward image, trying once again to do and be *just right*. The whole scene struck the same deep chords inside me.

I found that quite discouraging at first. I guess something in us longs to feel that we can untangle the jumbled strands inside us, once and for all. "There now, I'll never struggle with those old issues again." When we find ourselves relapsing into the same old patterns, there is a tendency to think that any progress we've made is an illusion. At least, that's the way I felt for a while.

Eventually, though, I realized that what I was up against was the nature of change as a process rather than an event. And part of any recovery process means that we embrace the journey involved. That "journey" is not a steady climb in a linear direction up a gently elevating slope. Progress, I discovered, follows more the pattern of a spiral where we recycle the same issues, but at a deeper level of understanding and personal choice.

Moving home to my roots allowed me to see that an inclination to some form of perfectionism and indispensability will always be a current issue for me. *Even more, there is value and worth in the struggle.* These issues form a personal backdrop against which I continue to realize my sin, my legitimate dependence, my incompleteness—and the grace of God. Against this background the two intractable realities of the gospel are brought together in my life: I am deeply flawed . . . and I am deeply loved.

BEING A PILGRIM

For years I have heard Christians referred to as "pilgrims." But whenever I thought of being one my mind got sidetracked by pictures of John Bunyan as a young boy dressed in peasant garb. Somehow I found it hard to apply the word to myself.

But being a pilgrim, I am discovering, is a matter of the heart, as Psalm 84 suggests. Blessed is the one whose heart is set on pilgrimage. A pilgrim is a woman whose children don't sit still through church, whose fingernails are in disrepair, whose desk badly needs organization. A pilgrim is one who is on the way. She's not there yet, not fixed, not complete, but she's following in the footsteps of One who promised to be with her in the midst of it all.

The more I read the Bible, the more I am impressed with how real the characters seem. They too were pilgrims. Their stories are lifted out of another time, another culture, but the main theme is always the same: They were individuals who struggled and stumbled and occasionally overcame, whose actual lives God entered.

God was present, at some points, by cloud and pillar of fire, patently apparent. He spoke through a donkey's lips and on words etched in stone—and most powerfully, through the cries of an infant in a manger. His story has been forever mingled with our own. He has not been, as I have sometimes supposed, standing back somewhere with His arms folded waiting for me to get my act together before He comes alongside.

I realize that the most, it seems, at the oddest of times. Like one of the impossible days when nothing goes right and my best hope is just to start over tomorrow with a new slate. I remember one recently, when by the day's end I had worked hard and yet still had nothing salvageable on paper. After weathering a fourteen-year-old's emotional storms, I decided I needed a remedial course on raising teenagers. The scales told me an unwelcome truth: I'd gained back the weight I lost.

As I climbed into bed that night, I reached for a novel I'd been reading. Then I thought, *What I really need is just to read a simple psalm before I turn out the light.* And yet, there is something about a really difficult day full of situations I haven't handled all that well that sometimes makes me want to do anything *but* open the Bible. This night, though, I turned to a psalm I have known by heart for twenty years and heard some of its words for the first time.

Psalm 73 is the diary of man named Asaph who must have had a string of bad days. It seemed to him, as it sometimes does to me, that everyone else had an easier go of it. The paragraph I read was this:

> My heart was embittered,
> And I was pierced within,
> ... I was senseless and ignorant;
> I was like a beast before Thee.
> Nevertheless I am continually with Thee;
> Thou hast taken hold of my right hand.
> With Thy counsel Thou wilt guide me,
> And afterward receive me to glory.
>   (verses 21-24, NASB)

The little word *nevertheless* is the one on which this passage hinges, I recognized. When Asaph was feeling his most beastly, his most ignorant, God was with him nevertheless.

My hand is held by One who knows the worst about me and yet refuses to turn away. He persists in loving me in those moments and on those days when I am least inclined toward that myself. The "nevertheless" in this passage reminds me that I am a pilgrim on a journey, a less-than-perfect woman who is being upheld in spite of herself—and who one day will be received into the glory of His presence.

BASIC PROVISIONS

If we continue to think of progress as a journey full of ups and downs, ins and outs, then a few basic provisions are important to keep in ample supply along the way. I think of these as natural antidotes to the tendency to live in a breathless rush consumed by the needs and demands around us. These natural remedies add balance and bring perspective. They serve to shorten the periods of feeling stuck in old self-defeating ways of living.

Real People

The nature and depth of our relationships is probably the most significant single factor in breaking free of patterns of perfectionism and indispensability.

At least a few faces in our minds need to qualify for the word *friend*. A real friend is someone who knows our story. A real friend is a fellow-pilgrim. She knows where we've come from, what we've struggled with, who the significant relations in our life are. When we share some new struggle or triumph, it doesn't fall into a void or become distorted by envy or contempt. There is a give-and-take to the relationship where we see each other's lives in a picture of continuity.

For most of us, if we are ever to move off the level of dangling conversations and superficial smiles, it will be because we really want something more. We want a real friend. And friendship takes time and the willingness to risk in order to build up a level of trust.

Close friendships hold the potential to be the brakes on a life that spins out of control at times. A good friend is like a mirror. If she loves you she'll know when to reflect the truth back to you, even when you are looking for something else.

Safe Places

A safe place is one where you can contribute without being measured by what you've achieved or provided in a tangible, performance-oriented way. It solicits the opposite of your normal inclinations.

Sally, the English teacher who critiques her husband's speeches, has begun to visit the women's prison in her hometown. At first she felt hopelessly out of place. Her graduate degrees meant nothing in that environment. Yet that was also part of what made those visits strangely restorative for Sally. In a very woman-to-woman way, the women she met were interested only in visiting with Sally herself. They didn't care how orderly she kept her closets or how well she could diagram a sentence.

It was an environment with no pretense where the pressure to perform was noticeably absent. Sally feels that prison draws her back to the things in life that are simple and unadorned. It invites her to consider the weak and broken places in her own life.

Each of us needs to cultivate a few places where just simply being there is a welcome relief and an invitation to "be" instead of to "do."

Simple Solitudes

There is something incredibly rejuvenating about silence and solitude. Down through the ages, wise men and women have understood this. Solitude is a pilgrim's refuge. Jesus, in the midst of a people-filled life, nevertheless said to His disciples, "Come with me by yourselves to a quiet place and get some rest" (Mark 6:31).

A friend recently told me that she had remodeled her house in order to have a small, private garden in the back. It was now complete, filled with flowers and a swing. "But you know what?" she said. "We go for weeks and never stop long enough to sit out there." That is so often the case. The opportunity to be alone gets passed up and, often with it, the very refreshment that would replenish our energies.

In the last few years, I have returned to my old habit of visiting a local monastery or convent for a few days about twice a year. I am always reminded by how cacophonous my normal life is when I have a few days without a telephone or radio or people talking to me. At first the silence is unnerving. But the longer I stay, the more rejuvenating it becomes.

What I enjoy most about those times is the absence of

an agenda. I take only the bare essentials with me—cheese and crackers, juice, a few clothes, my Bible, and a note pad. I let the time away evolve on its own: sleeping when I feel like sleeping, taking walks and praying, following different trails through God's Word than I normally would. What I find is that without concentrated effort and fore-thought, still I gain a perspective on the direction I'm being led and the courage to head there.

Play with No Purpose

For the woman who lives by appointments and a sched-ule, being able to let loose and do something frivolous and spontaneous is really important. And it's also helpful in restoring balance to our lives.

Leisure that is most restorative has a few key ingre-dients: It lacks tight schedules, deadlines, or hard-nosed competition. Once you are able to give yourself the per-mission to include a few things in your life out of pure enjoyment, the list of possibilities is endless. It can be as simple as a hobby of arranging fresh flowers. I've known women who quietly carve out a day on their calendar every so often and save it for doing only the things they simply *want* to do—go to an afternoon movie, have lunch with a friend, visit an art museum. Others invent little "mini-vacations," where for an hour or so, they step out of their normal routine and do something fun.

Once a woman sees the energizing, restorative quality to non-purposeful play, it moves out of the category of a luxury she doesn't have time for. It actually buys her time because it brings perspective.

New Risks

Being willing to take new risks is a mark of real growth for women who do too much. It means we are moving out of such tightly scripted patterns of perfectionism. It is evi-dence that the fear of failure and the need to do it right the first time are not so large and overwhelming.

Taking new risks is important because they induce us to move into the awkward, unsure places in life where self-sufficiency won't work. We have to learn new skills, new approaches, and that requires the help of others. All of a sudden, we're learners again, instead of teachers. This is the opposite of being superwomen.

Sometimes those risks come in the form of a new venture. Ellen, the woman whose mother orchestrated her and her sisters' achievements, is finding her entre-preneurial wings. She and a partner have launched a small human-resources consulting firm in Seattle. She knows she is a small fish in a large pond. But what she enjoys the most is the fresh challenge each day brings. "It's really been a growing experience for me to make an appointment with a company executive. There are days when I'm convinced that I just can't do this. And then I take a deep breath and pick up the phone," she says. "I'm growing from having to take risks."

Often those risks, though, are more relational in nature. We begin to spend time with people that we would nor-mally find uncomfortable. We share a struggle in our life that is still current and unfixed. We help a friend, knowing we can't take away her hurt, but we offer what we have to give.

These things, then—real people, safe places, simple solitudes, play without a purpose, and new risk—are some of the built-in safeguards that encourage us in the midst of this kind of pilgrimage.

MORE ORDINARY . . . MORE REAL

When my husband and I were dating we often stopped for ice cream after work. Those were the days when "31 flavors" were the big deal in ice cream, and I tried nearly every variety—often two or three different kinds on the same cone. Stacy always bought vanilla. Consistently, day after day, he chose vanilla over thirty other options. I asked him once how he could bear to eat vanilla when he could have had pralines 'n cream. And his response, the wisdom that I understand more all the time, was simply, "Paula, you don't realize how good this *vanilla* is."

Vanilla. It would never have occurred to me to appreciate the vanilla version of anything. That is the Achilles heel of the woman who does too much. The ordinary, the average, the everyday is viewed with contempt. When our senses are primarily attuned to the biggest or the brightest or the best, we miss an awful lot of life—real life. But as we let go of our driving need to be everything to everyone—to be perfect—a strange thing happens: We stumble on pleasure in simpler things.

It's amazing how much there is to enjoy in people if their success or table manners or response to you is not an indictment on your worth. All the little incidentals of life aren't just bumps in the road on the way to some big event. They are life, too. And something inside us opens to embrace them in a way that makes them new. A walk beneath a crisp blue sky, mastering broccoli soup, a belly laugh with a friend—the ordinary things become delights. The ordinary is extraordinary, if you no longer have to have the rush of constant adrenaline to feel alive, to feel like you're somebody.

Not long ago I returned from a trip and decided to sleep in late the next morning. The alarm went off and right before I was ready to get out of bed, Stacy, who'd just finished getting the kids' breakfast, came and crawled in beside me. I burrowed my face into the warmth of his sweater and rested for a long minute in the arc of his shoulder. It was such a warm feeling of being protected, a shelter of momentary respite from which to get up and face the day. The thought occurred to me, *A few years ago I would have given Stacy a quick peck on the cheek before*

I bounded out of bed in first gear.

Those moments of rest and pleasure were ones I would not have recognized, then, even when they were offered. Robert Fulghum uses a particular phrase to describe that mode of living. He refers to it as *standing knee deep in a river of water and dying of thirst.* The point being, of course, that there is often more available to us right where we are than we are willing or able to receive.

The journey out of the backwaters of compulsive living is really one of being relieved of the pressure from the past to be some form of superwoman in the present. The nod of approval we once looked for in our mother's face, and then a hundred faces after that, can't be replaced by a pay raise or a bigger house or smarter children. But it is possible to recapture the energy in that search for security and approval and steer it in more fruitful directions.

The quest of the woman who does too much is to live in the humility of being who she really is. To believe that God knew what He was doing when He made her. And that she is—this moment—the right age, the right gender, the right size. She has done enough. Or more accurately, she can never do enough to warrant the kind of love that's been offered her in Christ. She can only reach out and claim it.

A SPIRIT OF ADVENTURE

I used to think that by the time I turned forty, I would have a clear blueprint of my life. It was mostly a matter of growing older and wiser. But then I turned forty, and I had to admit I still didn't have it all together.

I had hoped that age would bring a light to my path the equivalent of Paul Revere's lantern, where the way would be certain. The illusion was that if I could find the sure path, I could bypass the rough, messy places in life. I could avoid real struggle or failure or pain. Reaching the phantom ideal of perfection, or finding a sure path, was the unnamed goal of much of my hard work and internal drive.

But I have grown older, and somewhere in the process I recognize that what I hold in my hand is more like a match. God allows me to take a few steps forward by that light. The path does not guarantee me a detour around the hard places. I'm not in control of the process—not really, anyway. The life of faith never loses its tentative feel. It never ceases to feel like faith. But what faith means to a woman like me, who has tried hard to orchestrate her life, to make it happen right, is that I begin to relax in the hand of One who leads the stars out at night and calls them all by name—*and yet cares for me.*

The incompleteness of real life continually leads me back to the stark simplicity of trusting God. And when I allow myself to relax in that, life with all its strange quirks, all its unpredictability, takes on the spirit of an adventure. I can experience the dark and light sides of life and gather the richness from both. I am able, as Sue Monk Kidd once wrote, to say "yes to life at the core of my being."[1]

The more I let go of my efforts to control life through hard work or pleasing others, the more human and dependent I see myself. Paradoxically, it is only in my rightful human proportions that I can appreciate how big God is. He is so much bigger than I thought. I see Him a little more as He is—big enough to encompass my meanderings, my doubt, and my helplessness, all the tattered edges of my life I so long to see made whole and right.

So many of the ought's and should's and have-to's of my life have been self-imposed; they spring from the twisted independence that places me at the center with everyone somehow crazily dependent on me. What God has offered me all along, and what you have to look over your do-list to see, I think, is a peculiar kind of freedom. It's the freedom of being able to serve Him *because He doesn't need me.* He is about His business in a world that He died for, and the wonder of it all is that He lets me have a small part. He lets me come along. What looks like duty is, in reality, far closer to privilege.

God invites me into a relationship that moves from the old status of His enemy to a new one, as His daughter in Christ. For years I've lived more like a hired woman, who would be dismissed summarily if she sat down on the job—or promoted and blessed if she performed up to standard.

But being a daughter is a different relationship altogether. A daughter may grieve her Father, she may encounter His discipline, but she has the basic confidence of belonging and being loved.[2] A daughter can work and serve and give—and a daughter can play and rest and receive. When we begin to embrace that reality—that we live as God's daughters by grace—we have the emotional means of letting go of our overwrought efforts to control and manage life on our own.

As women who are so prone to do and achieve, to help and to please, we are peculiarly attuned to the whole notion of perfection. Our truest instincts lead us to reach for more than we can ever know this side of Heaven. And if we follow those desires to their true source, we will discover Him.

In the deepest parts of our souls we are all brides, celibate and unfilled, waiting for that day when we will be reunited with our Bridegroom, completed beyond all our wildest hopes. Someday—not now, but someday—the perfection and glory we desire will no longer be an unreachable ideal.

They will be ours—because we share His.[3]

NOTES

1. Sue Monk Kidd, *When the Heart Waits* (San Francisco: Harper & Row, 1990), page 184.
2. David Seamands, *Healing Grace* (Wheaton: Victor Books, 1989), page 23.
3. 1 John 3:1-3.

AUTHOR

Paula Rinehart is a writer whose nonfiction books reflect a focused interest in people, what hinders and helps them. She is the coauthor (with her husband) of the award-winning best seller *Choices*. She has also written a variety of articles for magazines such as *Christianity Today, Marriage Partnership*, and *Discipleship Journal*. She enjoys speaking on topics of critical concern to women—stress, mid-life transition, and personal growth. After fifteen years in the Midwest, Paula now lives in Raleigh, North Carolina, with her husband, Stacy, and their two children, Allison and Brady.